The Girl's Guide to Growing Your Own

The Girl's Guide to Growing Your Own

HOW TO GROW FRUIT AND VEGETABLES WITHOUT GETTING YOUR HANDS TOO DIRTY

ALEX MITCHELL

NEW HOLLAND

First published in 2009 by
New Holland Publishers (UK) Ltd
London · Cape Town · Sydney · Auckland

Garfield House
86-88 Edgware Road
London, W2 2EA
United Kingdom
www.newhollandpublishers.com

80 McKenzie Street
Cape Town 8001
South Africa

Unit 1, 66 Gibbes Street
Chatswood, NSW 2067
Australia

218 Lake Road
Northcote, Auckland
New Zealand

1 3 5 7 9 10 8 6 4 2

ISBN 978 1 84773 510 2

Editors: Amy Corstorphine and Jo Murray
Design: Lucy Parissi
Production: Laurence Poos
Editorial Direction: Rosemary Wilkinson
Illustrations: Nila Aye at New Division
Photography: Edward Alwright
Cover photography: David Hews
Additional photos: iStock Photo

Reproduction by Modern Age Repro House, Hong Kong
Printed and bound in India by Replika Press Pvt. Ltd

Contents

Introduction

I wasn't always the sort to wax lyrical over a lettuce leaf. A typical British child of the 1970s – the dawn of convenience food – I grew up eating boil-in-the-bag cod and baked beans. The nearest my mother got to growing her own peas was the frozen food aisles of our local supermarket. Now I eulogize cherry tomatoes, ponder over various types of kale and am never happier than when wandering round my tiny garden picking sun-warmed strawberries. What on earth happened? Was it was a reaction to living in a flat in north London in my mid-twenties, where the only wildlife was manky pigeons and the only greenery the plane trees in the street below? I started with window boxes of garish orange marigolds and red geraniums. Soon I graduated to rocket (arugula) and baby salad leaves. By the time I'd eaten my first home-grown tomato, I was hopelessly hooked.

As a journalist working on a tabloid newspaper alongside shouty, hard-drinking, hard-smoking hacks, I'd juggle my tomato growing bags with newspaper deadlines and keep my horticultural obsession quiet.

Ten or so years later and my passion for growing lovely things I can eat shows no sign of slowing down. But I'm no longer alone. Now I can hold my head high. We appear to be in the grip of a growing-your-own food revolution. And this time it's not only gentlemen of a certain age who are waxing lyrical over potatoes and aubergines (eggplants), but a whole cross section of society, many of them women, many of whom still have their own teeth.

Why? We've now had a few years of enjoying exotic fruit in winter, strawberries all year round and little French (green) beans lined up in perfect rows,

trimmed for our convenience and flown in from Kenya. Yet something doesn't feel right. What about food miles, pesticides, packaging, organic food standards, the state of the farming industry? What's in those bagged salads? Most of all, what about taste? We've all eaten things that looked like strawberries, but tasted like, well, nothing at all. And when did peaches start resembling cotton wool?

Yet what's a modern, urban-living, eco-conscious girl to do? You might want to eat local, fresher, organically grown fruit and vegetables, but you don't want to move to the middle of nowhere, embrace a collection of headscarves and become self-sufficient. You could get an allotment, but even if you managed to get to the top of the waiting list before you're too old to lift a hand trowel, you might not want the hassle of travelling to a large plot some distance from your home that will need your attention come rain or shine the whole year round. You don't want to break your back digging and lugging heavy sacks or rigging up complicated wooden supports or nets. You might not want to spend every weekend in a rickety shed cradling a glass of someone else's nettle wine. You want to carry on as you are thanks, just with fewer trips to the supermarket and the pleasure of picking and eating your own fresh, organic produce with the minimum of effort.

This is the book I wish I'd had when I started growing my own. It's not for gardening nuts, it's for people who have a busy life, but still like the idea of eating a fresh salad they've grown themselves, popping outside to get some herbs for a risotto or eating deliciously ripe strawberries straight off the plant. How often do you see blue potatoes, stripy tomatoes, golden beetroot (beet), yellow mangetout (snow peas) or purple French (green) beans at your supermarket? Or, for that matter, trombone-shaped squashes, purple artichokes and white aubergines (eggplants) flecked with the most delicate pink? You don't need a greenhouse or any fancy equipment to grow any of the plants in this book. With just a hand trowel, some seedlings, a few pots and a bag of compost you can conjure a veritable harvest from a balcony or even a couple of windowsills. If you get yourself some nice gardening gloves – I defy anyone to say my pink-trimmed suede gauntlets are not objects of beauty – you won't even need to break a nail.

So what do you want to grow?

Some crops are easier to grow than others. Sometimes I think you could throw rocket (arugula) seed into the wind and come back three weeks later and find a salad. Aubergines (eggplants), on the other hand, can refuse to crop unless they're showered with love and proverbial fan mail. To make it easier to choose what you might want to grow, I've only included crops that are easy to grow in small gardens and pots. I have, however, included a few

demanding divas. And when the result could be a warm, sun-ripened peach, a bowl of purple figs or a sweet roasted red pepper, the rewards are worth it.

Symbols explained

You couldn't kill it if you tried

Reliable favourites – the horticultural equivalent of the little black dress

Won't be taken for granted, but no diva either

Fussy but fabulous

Cheat's Tip

Weekend Project

Recipe

Getting started

DON'T I NEED TO BUY LOTS OF TOOLS?

No. There will always be people – by which I mean men – who draw outlines of spades, hoes and forks on their garden shed walls so they can hang their vast collection of tools in exactly the right place in order that they don't get mixed up or, God forbid, actually touch the floor. This is a conspiracy to make women think gardening is complicated so they won't interrupt men when they're hiding in their sheds. Here's the news, you don't need lots of tools and you really don't need a shed.

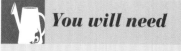

You will need

For seed sowing, I use either small 7.5 cm (3 in) plastic pots or module trays – plastic grids of interconnected cells available from any garden centre. These are great because, when it's time to transplant the seedlings, you just pop out the cell and plant the whole thing, so you don't have to worry about damaging the roots. Labels are good for reminding you what you've sown where (I'm constantly seeing lettuces poke up where peas should have been) and garden twine always comes in useful. Otherwise, those gardening in containers can do everything they need with a hand trowel, some nice pots and a watering can with a rose attachment (a perforated spout). Those with a garden will need a garden fork and spade, too. Everything can be purchased online or bought on a quick trip to a garden centre.

CROPS IN POTS

Most fruit and vegetable crops can be grown in pots – in fact, some, like figs and blueberries, prefer it. A group of plants in containers can look as jungly as a garden border and you can fit in masses on a small terrace, from herbs to fruit trees. In fact, pretty much any crop can be grown in a pot, if it's big enough. If you treat them as mini beds, cramming in different plants – salad leaves, courgettes (zuccinis) and nasturtiums, say, or purple French (green) beans and Californian poppies at the base of a fig tree – pots can look surprisingly lush. Large terracotta pots, weathered with lichen, can be objects of beauty in themselves.

The best thing about growing in containers, though, is that you don't have to worry about your

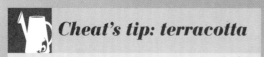

Cheat's tip: terracotta

Old terracotta pots – with their faded charm and patina of lichen and calcification – are so much more appealing than the brand new, orange, machine-made ones. For a start, they make it look like you've been gardening for ages so actually know what you're doing. To speed up the ageing process, paint some natural yogurt onto the new pots. It encourages lichen and moss to grow on them and no one will ever know you didn't inherit them from dear old grandpapa's estate.

soil because you're not using it. Just buy some organic multipurpose compost to fill your pots with and you're good to go. And if you haven't time even to sow crops, you can buy them as seedlings and plant them straight out. It's pretty much instant gardening.

Any container can be used to grow plants in as long as it has holes in the base for water to drain away. You could use an ice-cream tub if you wanted, though you may not thrill to the idea of a terrace full of things with Mint Choc Chip written on the side. If so, there are many options…

Terracotta: Terracotta is classy and pots look better every year. Handmade terracotta pots are gorgeous although they can be pricey, while the machine-made ones are a snip but usually come in a disconcerting orange. Don't dismiss them, though, there's a way to beautify them…

Glazed pots: These pots are for people who want to pretend they live in the Mediterranean, which is most of us. They usually come in deep vivid blues, turquoises and greens.

Metal containers: Metal containers – for those aiming for a clean, modern look – work really well, whether galvanized tin, copper, zinc, aluminium or brushed steel.

Fibreclay pots: Fibreclay pots are also available, and are styled to look like lead. Light, large and deep enough for fruit trees, they look just like those heavy lead planters you see in the gardens of stately homes with the bonus that you don't have to remortgage your house to buy them and they won't fall into your downstairs neighbour's breakfast.

Cheat's tip: three's a crowd

For some reason odd numbers of containers always look better than even ones – the same rule applies when planting seedlings out in the garden. Three or five plants make a nice cluster – a group of two or four looks contrived and unnatural.

Pretty in pink

I'm never entirely sure about the marketing principle that anything aimed at women has to be pink and flowery, but it's nice not to have to look like your granddad when you're planting your Charlotte potatoes. These days, there's a huge range of girly gardening accessories out there to bring the ladylike to your labours. Whether it's a pair of pink-trimmed, suede pruning gauntlets, some kitsch wellington boots, a linen, flowery kneeling cushion, or a set of shiny hand tools so diddy you'll want to put them on your mantelpiece, you can now wildly indulge your feminine side when tending your salad. There are also ladylike ranges of lighter, smaller garden forks and spades. They haven't put pink flowers on these yet, but give them time. *See Little Green Book, page 140.*

Old wooden wine crates: These are lovely for salad crops – ask at your nearest wine merchants, they often have some they're throwing out. They're somehow the perfect size to grow a decent patch of greens or even tomatoes and their imprinted logos give them a certain élan.

I love brightly coloured pots – orange, shocking pink and yellow – planted up with chillies or tomatoes. You can also get really cute little bag pots, made from reclaimed vegetable sacks *(see Little Green Book, page 140).*

Or feel free to improvise. If you're feeling creative you can use anything – colanders, hats, teapots, even old boots – as growing containers. I've even

Cheat's tip: sprinkle with shingle

Make crops in pots look the business by covering the top of the compost with a layer of shingle. It not only looks smart and reflects light, hiding all that dark earth, but also keeps moisture in the compost so reduces the amount of watering you need to do. A medium-sized bag of pea shingle is easy to find in garden centres and goes a very long way.

seen strawberries growing happily in a leather handbag. Old butler sinks are popular but beware, they are incredibly heavy – and do add plenty of crocks and grit at the bottom since the plug hole may not be enough for drainage. Some people seem to like the challenge of turning any old incongruous thing into a container. Tyres, buckets, old baths … I'm still scarred by memories of a friend who kept planting lobelia in a toilet. I sometimes think there's a fine line between creativity and a lay-by that's recently been fly-tipped.

Hanging baskets

Cheery they might be, but stylish? Long the preserve of the British pub, hanging baskets are traditionally the antithesis of restraint, bursting out all over with clashing busy lizzies, geraniums and marigolds like an over-exuberant hat. Plant them up with edibles, however, and a whole new world of possibilities is opened up. 'Tumbler' tomatoes, peas, alpine strawberries, salad and herbs all love growing in hanging baskets out of reach of pests.

If you don't want a traditional-style basket for fear of turning your house into Ye Olde Twee Arms Public House, feel free to get creative with brightly coloured tins and bits of string. Choose the tin wisely, though. There's a big difference between hanging up a charming Greek olive oil can planted with oregano and bunging some lettuce in a tin of super-saver baked beans.

Go, Growing Bags

They may be unfashionable, but I love growing bags. Long, plastic-wrapped sausages of compost, they're usually emblazoned with garish pictures of tomatoes and don't look very chic. However stylish your collection of weathered terracotta pots is, bung a growing bag in there and you'll really lower the tone. And yet they're so perfect for growing tomatoes in a small space that I use them every year. Nothing is easier than making three crosses in the plastic with a kitchen knife and then planting a tomato in each. They always seem to thrive, even if plants in the soil or other pots struggle.

But how to deal with that plastic? In an unusually industrious/creative moment, I had some shallow wooden boxes made, just the right size to fit the bags in. I then covered the bags with shingle so you'd never know they were there. You can now buy similar boxes ready-made from garden equipment suppliers *(see Little Green Book, page 140)*. Alternatively, display your garish, plastic growing bags with pride and tell anyone who criticizes them not to be such a terrible snob.

Window boxes

Most people, even those who live in flats, have a garden. It's just that it might be three floors up and on your windowsill. Outdoor window ledges are great growing spaces. All you need is a window box.

I tend to avoid plastic window boxes because, however glorious the plants in them, all I can see is the ugly box. Terracotta and light metal ones always look good, wooden ones are great for a rustic look and there are rattan ones for the folksy-devoted. But my current favourites are those made of fibreclay styled to look like lead, large enough to hold plants like aubergines (eggplants) and peppers. Whatever you

Cheat's tip: hanging baskets

The only problem with hanging baskets is that they dry out quickly in hot weather. Regular watering is therefore essential, but to make life a bit easier mix a handful of water-retaining gel into the compost when you plant them.

choose get the biggest and deepest you can for your windowsill (weight restrictions permitting). Small, shallow boxes can dry out in a few hours on a hot summer's day – the larger the box, the less you'll be rushing back and forth with a watering can.

The heavier the window box, the less likely it is to blow off and knock someone out in the street below, but it's worth taking precautions however much you may dislike your downstairs neighbours. You can buy handy bracket and box kits that keep everything safely tethered or tie a sturdy chain around the box and attach it to the wall and sleep better on those windy nights.

GROWING IN GARDEN SOIL

Yes, I know, this is the boring bit. Can't I just plant something in the earth as it is and hope for the best, you might be thinking? Well, you can, but you might not get very many tomatoes in return. I don't know, perhaps you have inherited your garden from a lovely old gent who has spent the past 40 years digging in manure, clearing weeds and removing stones, leaving you with perfect soil that you can merely touch with a seed and cause a productive, edible jungle to grow. But it's highly unlikely. Chances are your garden, like most gardens, is a green rectangle of boggy lawn flanked by borders of limping shrubs, badly drained soil, a healthy army of weeds and an abandoned bicycle (why do all gardens seem to contain an abandoned bicycle?).

So how do you transform it into a verdant paradise of tomatoes, sweetcorn, salad and beans?

Cheat's tip: a silver lining

Metal window boxes are light and modern, but they tend to heat up in hot weather. This dries out the compost and can overheat the roots. Insulate the box against the sun by lining the inside (not bottom) of the box with any sheets of polystyrene you might have hanging around from packaging.

Love your loam

It's a gardener's maxim, often muttered by allotment veterans and other know-it-alls that 'look after your soil and the plants will look after themselves'. They have a point. The first step to getting your soil ready to plant into is to find out what sort it is.

Pick up a small handful and try to form it into a ball shape between your palms. If it won't form a ball and feels gritty, it's sandy; if you can form it into

a thick cylinder but not a thread, it's silty; if you can form it into a ring, then it's clay; if you can't form it into any shape at all, then it's a patio.

Sandy soil: Sandy soils have large particles and, like sand on a beach, allow water to drain through quickly. This means that they warm up quickly in the spring so you can start planting earlier than those with other soils. They are also light to dig so your back will thank you. On the downside, nutrients get washed out of them so you need to add organic matter to slow this down as well as to prevent them drying out in hot weather. Generally, though, this is one of the easiest soils to deal with, so well done you.

Silty soil: If your soil is silty it will contain more nutrients than sandy soil yet still drain well. When dry, silty soils are smooth and look like dark sand. They are easy to work with when moist and hold moisture well but benefit from the addition of grit and organic matter.

Clay soil: Clay soil is often described as a 'challenge', which is another way of saying, 'poor you'. However, if treated properly it can be the most fertile of all soils so persevere and you'll be rewarded. To understand why clay soil has this rather fearsome reputation, imagine digging a lump of sticky, wet clay with a trowel. It's the tiny particles that make up clay soil that make it so heavy since there is very little room for air pockets. When wet, it is very sticky; when dry it forms rock-hard clods. But, and here's the good news, clay soils naturally contain high levels of nutrients. So, if you can improve the drainage, you are on to a winner. Adds lots of sharp sand or grit and organic matter – manure or garden compost.

Chalky soil: Soil that is chalky is alkaline, light brown and contains large quantities of stones. Basically, chalky soils are a bit rubbish, but not irredeemable. They dry out quickly and have a tendency to stop elements such as iron and manganese getting to plants, which can cause poor growth and yellow leaves. Add lots of organic matter.

Cheat's tip: raised bed kits

If you can't face preparing your soil for planting, there is a way out. Most garden equipment suppliers (*see Little Green Book, page 140*) sell raised bed kits, basically shallow wooden or plastic squares that you fill with compost or topsoil. They work like giant containers and mean you don't have to be so vigilant about your garden soil since you're raising the level a good few centimetres. Just break up the earth at soil level before you put the raised bed on so you don't compromise drainage.

Raised bed kits are popular because they give the impression of instant gardening and look very neat and tidy. However, you will have to construct them so factor in some time and hassle. They also scream 'Vegetable Plot!' so, if you're aiming for a more organic, mix-n-match look, combining flowers and vegetables in a potager style, they may not be for you.

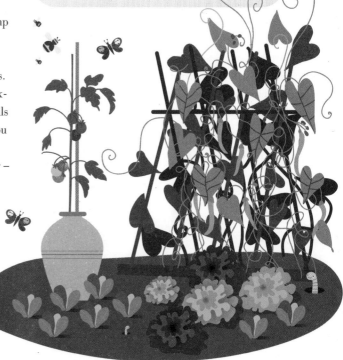

Loamy soil: This is the crème de la crème of garden soils, the Olympic Gold of the earth world. A winning combination of sand, silt and clay, loamy soil combines good drainage with an ability to hold on to nutrients well. If you have been working your garden soil for years, adding well-rotted manure and garden compost regularly, you may well have one of these soils. In which case, I envy you.

The great news is that all soils are redeemable with the addition of well-rotted farmyard manure or garden compost, both of which come under the general category of organic matter.

Garden compost

'My whole life has been spent waiting for an epiphany, a manifestation of God's presence, the kind of transcendent, magical experience that lets you see our place in the big picture. And that is what I had with my first compost heap.'
Bette Midler

And who am I to argue with a diva? Forget yoga, meditation, even the power of a luxury department store card, it seems that spiritual peace was always waiting for us in the shape of bits of old carrot. Who knew? Ever since I threw potato peelings, coffee grounds, dead plants and slug-eaten lettuce leaves into a compost bin and got crumbly soil stuff out a year later, I've been a total composting maniac. Put the stuff on your garden and it makes everything grow bigger and better. It's organic, it's easy and it's phenomenally satisfying in a circle-of-life kind of way.

Why would I want a smelly plastic thing cluttering up my garden when I've got a perfectly good rubbish collection service, you might think? My answer to this is that compost doesn't smell if you jab a garden fork into it now and then, and that my two white clapboard 'beehive'-style compost bins are more stylish than my sofa – though that may say more about my sofa than my compost bins.

Manure: What do you mean you don't know the whereabouts of your nearest defecating horse?

I did a garden course once in which the teacher mentioned well-rotted garden manure approximately every six minutes, like a sort of horticultural Tourette's. 'Spread well-rotted garden manure over your soil in autumn,' he would say, or 'Be sure to incorporate plenty of well-rotted manure.' (For some reason, manure is always 'incorporated' in garden

from garden centres in nice, clean plastic bags. There are also online companies that will deliver manure. But make sure it's a responsible company. A friend once opened the door to a smiling man offering well-rotted manure for sale. How nice, she thought, and got out her wallet. Ten minutes later a heap of steaming, stinking fresh manure was dumped all over her front garden. She spread it on her beds where it burned all the plants, turning the leaves yellow, so proving the maxim, never trust a man with dirty shoes.

Dig for victory

This is the sort of thing that some gardeners get very vexed about. I don't want to generalize but, OK, they're mostly men. They spend whole weekends digging trenches that reach almost as far as Australia (this is known as 'double digging') and carefully sorting soil into topsoil and subsoil. They may also have garden sheds that they love only slightly less than their wives. Really, and I'm going to stick my neck out here, unless you're unfortunate enough to be gardening on a paddock compressed by a herd of cattle for the past ten years – double digging is unnecessary.

Much better to find a free 40 minutes and isolate a manageable area – perhaps nothing more than a square metre to start with. Dig down to the depth of a garden fork, removing any weeds and stones and breaking up lumps in the soil with the back of the fork. Then, if you have a clay soil that doesn't drain well, dig in some garden grit (a couple of shovelfuls per square metre – available from all garden centres). If not, just spread a layer of manure or compost about 10 cm (4 in) thick on the top and fork it in. Ideally, you'd put the compost or manure on in the autumn and let it settle into the soil a bit before planting in spring, but any time of year is OK.

It's a material world

When I started this gardening lark there were times I thought I'd inadvertently wandered into a builder's merchants. What did sharp sand and horticultural

books, as though it's joining a company.) Even if I knew what this stuff was, I'd wonder, how can I locate it in an urban area when sightings of horses and cows are about as common as a street without a Starbucks? And how rotted is 'well rotted'?

Basically, if it doesn't smell, it's well rotted. It's the manure of horses or cows mixed in with straw and left to rot down for at least a year, preferably two or three. When you add it to the soil it helps water drain through and adds nutrients, particularly nitrogen, which promotes healthy green growth, as well as phosphorus and potassium, which stimulate root growth and fruit production. If you don't let it rot down first, it'll burn the plants and smell like a herd of cows has just used your garden as a lavatory, which in essence, they just have.

Before you set off in search of a police horse to walk behind carrying a large plastic container, you should know that you can buy well-rotted manure grit have to do with pretty flowers and perfect raspberries? As for perlite, why would you put the contents of your beanbag in a vegetable bed?

Now I'm older and a little bit wiser I know grit and sharp sand are added to heavy soils, such as clay, to let water drain through better and not waterlog the roots of plants. Sharp sand is used because it's quite coarse grained, so allows water to run through it better than finer varieties. Don't use beach or children's sandpit sand because they contain salts that damage plants. Horticultural grit works in a similar way, opening up the soil and letting water drain through. If you have a heavy clay garden soil *(see Love your loam, page 14)* it's worth a trip to a garden centre or DIY superstore to get a bag or two of either.

Perlite, which looks like little polystyrene balls although it's actually made of volcanic rock, does the same thing but is used when planting in pots. It's worth adding a handful to the compost when you're planting things that hate being waterlogged, such as Mediterranean herbs, or those that will stay in the same pot for ages, like fruit trees.

Soil preparation in a nutshell

1 Work out what sort of garden soil you have *(see Love your loam, page 14)*

2 Turn over about a garden fork's depth of soil, removing weeds and large stones and breaking up clods so you get a fine, crumbly texture

3 Fork in grit or sand if you have a clay or silty soil

4 Add a thick layer (at least 10 cm/4 in) of well-rotted manure or garden compost, loosely digging it into the earth

5 Have a nice cup of tea. Right, now that's all sorted, you're ready to actually plant something.

Spring

Kick off your shoes, get out your sunglasses, spring has sprung. Actually, on second thoughts, don't. The sun may be higher in the sky and new leaves unfurling, but spring can seem to take an agonizingly long time to get going. I used to get so excited at the first glimpse of a green leaf that I'd skip around the garden in a T-shirt, sowing beetroot (beet), carrots and lettuce and pretending I wasn't getting hypothermia. Unsurprisingly, all the seed rotted and died. It's better – and, let's face it, far less hassle – to sow a few things on a warm windowsill inside, nice and cosy, and plant them when you can go outside without your fingers going numb.

From early spring, beetroot (beet), lettuces and chard can be started off in module trays or little plastic pots inside. You can also lay out your potatoes to start chitting (*see 'Jargon buster' p.37*). By mid spring, it's time to plant potatoes, sow tomatoes, courgettes (zucchinis), cucumbers, sweetcorn, basil, French (green) beans and peas inside and carrots, rocket (arugula) and radishes out. Don't feel you have to sow everything, turn your bathroom into a jungle and crunch compost underfoot every time you get into the bath. A few pots are more than enough. There's only so much chard anyone can eat, after all. And, if sowing sounds too much like hard work, you can always buy ready-grown plants from garden centres or online in late spring (*see Little Green Book, page 140*).

By the end of the season, the garden is raring to go. You might be eating your first succulent baby broad (fava) beans in a warm salad with tiny new potatoes, roast mini beetroot (beet) and feta. There's earthy kale for picking, refreshing radishes, fiery red radicchio, salad onions (scallions), cut-and-come-again salad, spicy rocket (arugula), chard, crunchy winter purslane and corn salad. On warm days you can almost hear the plants growing.

If you do only three things this season...

Plant salad potatoes, sow rocket (arugula), sow lettuce

salad potatoes

rocket (arugula)

lettuce

Rocket (Arugula)

DIFFICULTY RATING

Sowing rocket (arugula)

When? Mid-spring to late summer

In pots

YOU WILL NEED

A medium-sized container with drainage holes, multipurpose compost, rocket (arugula) seeds, 20 minutes

How? Add a layer of crocks to the bottom of the container and then fill it almost to the top with compost. Sprinkle the seeds thinly over the surface, then cover with a thin layer of compost. Water. Place in a sunny or partially shaded spot.

In garden soil

YOU WILL NEED

A pencil or stick, rocket (arugula) seeds, 10 minutes

How? Choose a sunny or partially shaded spot with well-cultivated soil. With your pencil or stick, scratch a shallow groove in the soil. Sprinkle the rocket (arugula) seed thinly along it, then cover with soil and water well.

What next? Keep moist and harvest leaves with scissors by cutting just above the smallest new leaf when the plants reach about 10 cm (4 in) tall. The plants will then resprout two or three times before needing to be resown.

Where have I gone wrong? Flea beetle is the only real pest of rocket (arugula) *(see Edible Garden Enemies, page 134).*

Hard to believe, I know, but we did once eat salads without this peppery little leaf. These days, every supermarket salad bag contains it, a restaurant garnish isn't complete without it and even pizzas come crowned with the stuff. We're addicted to rocket (arugula). Lucky it's so easy to grow then.

Sow it outside from mid-spring, straight into the pot or bit of ground you want to grow it in. It's super fast and needs no special attention. Rocket (arugula) basically comes in two types: salad rocket (arugula), with its more rounded leaves and less peppery taste, and the hotter wild rocket (arugula) with narrower, serrated leaves. I grow both. Sow little and often, though. If your rocket starts tasting like someone's poured hot mustard powder into your mouth and your eyes start streaming, it's time to pull up the plants and start again.

Radishes

They're the sprinters of the vegetable world yet radishes are easy to dismiss. I always used to put them in the category of things schoolchildren might grow in 'Veg Corner' – 'Good boy, Milo, look what you grew!' – but actually, a few crisp radishes sliced into a salad or sandwich or just eaten whole can be delicious. Best thing of all, though, is that they're one of the earliest crops you can harvest. 'French Breakfast' is long enough for slicing, with a pretty white tip. Real show offs would go for a packet of multicoloured 'Bright Lights' and pep up their salads with red, white, purple and even yellow ones.

Sowing radishes

When? From mid-spring

In pots

YOU WILL NEED

 A container with drainage holes, multipurpose compost, radish seeds, 20 minutes

How? Add a layer of crocks to the bottom of the container and then fill it almost to the top with compost. Sprinkle the seeds on the top, about 3 cm (1 in) apart, then cover with 1 cm (1/2 in) of compost. Water. Place in a sunny or partially shaded spot.

In garden soil

YOU WILL NEED

A pencil or stick, radish seeds, 10 minutes

How? Choose a sunny or partially shaded spot with well-cultivated soil. With your pencil or stick, scratch a shallow groove in the soil. Sprinkle the radish seed along it about 3 cm (1 in) apart, then cover with soil and water well.

What next? Keep moist. After about three weeks, investigate how big the radish bulbs have become and pull them up when you like the look of them.

Keep sowing every few weeks for a constant supply of radishes throughout the summer.

Salad onions (Scallions)

DIFFICULTY RATING

Snip them onto warm potatoes, salads or into sandwiches, spruce up a tuna mayonnaise or add to baked potato fillings ... salad or spring onions (scallions) are super versatile in the kitchen and easy-peasy to grow. 'White Lisbon' or 'Spring Slim' are good varieties for both open ground and containers. A row of onions sown at the front of a window box and backed by lettuces and nasturtiums looks very perky.

Sowing salad onions (scallions)
When? Mid-spring to midsummer

In pots

YOU WILL NEED
A medium-sized container with drainage holes, multipurpose compost, onion seeds, 20 minutes

How? Add a layer of crocks to the bottom of the container and then fill it almost to the top with compost. Sprinkle the seeds thinly over the surface, then cover with a thin layer of compost. Water. Place in a sunny or partially shaded spot.

In garden soil

YOU WILL NEED
A pencil or stick, onion seeds, 10 minutes

How? Choose a sunny or partially shaded spot with well-cultivated soil. With your pencil or stick, scratch a shallow groove in the soil. Sprinkle the onion seed thinly along it, then cover with soil and water well.
What next? Keep moist. Investigate how big the onion bulbs have become, pull them up when you like the look of them and add them to salads.

Cheat's tip: crocks away

Every time you plant anything in a pot or window box, you'll hear about adding 'crocks' to the bottom first. What on earth are they and do you really need to bother? Traditionally, they're bits of broken terracotta pot that stop the drainage holes from getting clogged up with compost and roots and waterlogging the plants. So, they are kind of necessary. But why would you want to smash a perfectly good pot? In ye olde times, large gardens might have had a constant supply of smashed terracotta (along with a constant supply of gardeners in braces and waistcoats), but these days, with a small garden, you probably don't have any. I use a couple of handfuls of garden shingle or gravel instead, along with any broken plastic pots. Stones are fine too. Or chuck in some broken up pieces of polystyrene. They're light, you can use them again and again and, best of all, you'll get rid of some of that damn packaging that's been cluttering up your hall.

Kale and Chorizo Soup

In early spring, when nothing much is growing, kale is a bit of a star in the garden, shrugging off the gloom. It's one of those vegetables that tastes like it's doing really good things to you. Counteract all this health with some self-indulgent chorizo for a simple, tasty broth.

Serves 4
2 tbsp olive oil
1 large onion, chopped
3 garlic cloves, crushed
250 g (8 oz) chorizo, sliced
1 litre (1½ pints) chicken or vegetable stock
sea salt and freshly ground black pepper
3 large potatoes, peeled and cubed
200 g (7 oz) kale

Heat the oil in a large saucepan. Add the onions, garlic and chorizo, then cook for a few minutes until the onion is soft. Pour in the stock, season and bring to the boil. Add the potato cubes and simmer for ten minutes. Meanwhile, wash and finely slice the kale. Add to the pan and simmer for another five minutes. Serve in bowls with warm, crusty bread.

Lettuce

DIFFICULTY RATING

Didn't lettuces used to be round, limp and the consistency of chamois leather? They did in the 1970s, when a salad meant half a hard-boiled egg, some rock-hard tomatoes and a few leaves of the green stuff, all smothered with salad cream so vinegary it threatened your taste buds with eviction. How things change. These days, we're more likely to be eating Lollo Rossa than Iceberg, and the good old round lettuce has become almost fashionably retro. Frilly, crisp, red, green, blousy, pointy, frou-frou or plain, it's a lettuce wonderland out there. Once you've eaten your own fresh lettuce, you'll never look at the chlorinated, supermarket pillow packs in the same way again.

Sow little and often and you can have fresh lettuce all year round. Whether it's a window box studded with five red and green oak-leafs, a hanging basket out of reach of snails or a few pots of mixed baby leaves on a balcony, lettuces are great for small spaces. Try them in a wooden wine crate (*see page 10*) – salad leaves look rather stylish growing above a logo for Chateauneuf du Pape. Or intersperse different-coloured lettuces in a chequerboard patch in a garden bed edged with spiky mizuna or rocket (arugula).

Either grow them to maturity and cut the whole thing, or sow them closer together and harvest with scissors above the smallest new leaf when they're still small. They'll resprout two or three times.

My favourite varieties are 'Red Oak Leaf' and 'Green Oak Leaf', great either for baby leaves or mature heads, frilly 'Lollo Rossa' and 'Lollo Bianca', and the sword-like 'Cocarde'. 'Little Gem' and 'Tom Thumb' are particularly good for growing in pots and bring a lovely, sweet crunchiness to sandwiches and salads. If you can't decide which varieties to buy, get a mixed packet and grow them as baby leaves.

 Cheat's tip: salad in a spin

Do yourself a favour, buy a salad spinner. When you've spent years buying ready-prepared salad in bags it can be easy to forget that you actually might have to wash the stuff before eating. You don't need to eat waterlogged salad. A simple, plastic salad spinner gives you crisp, dry leaves in a few seconds.

Sowing lettuce for baby leaves

Lettuce grown in this way is great for all containers – from window boxes to hanging baskets. Simply snip after a few weeks and watch it regrow. You can buy some lovely mixed baby lettuce leaf selections, with all sorts of different shaped and coloured leaves. **When?** Mid-spring to early autumn.

In pots

YOU WILL NEED

A medium-sized container with drainage holes, multipurpose compost, lettuce seeds, 20 minutes

How? Add a layer of crocks to the bottom of the container and then fill it almost to the top with compost. Sprinkle the seeds thinly over the surface, then cover with a thin layer of compost. Water. Place in a sunny or partially shaded spot.

In garden soil

YOU WILL NEED

A pencil or stick, lettuce seeds, 10 minutes

How? Choose a sunny or partially shaded spot with well-cultivated soil. With your pencil or stick, scratch a shallow groove in the soil. Sprinkle the lettuce seed thinly along it, then cover with a thin layer of soil. Alternatively, sprinkle seed thinly wherever a gap appears in your bed and cover with a handful of multipurpose compost. Water well.

What next? Keep moist and harvest leaves with scissors by cutting just above the smallest new leaf when the plants reach about 10 cm (4 in) tall. The plants will then resprout two or three times before needing to be resown.

For mature lettuces

Baby leaves are all very well, but you sometimes want some crunch in a salad, something with a heart. Grow lettuces to maturity and you can either harvest the whole thing at once or cut the outer leaves for sandwiches and salads as and when you want them. If you want a constant supply throughout the summer, resow when your seedlings have four leaves.

YOU WILL NEED

A module tray, multipurpose compost, lettuce seeds, 30 minutes

Where? In a module tray (a grid of plastic cells available from all garden centres). For spring sowings, pop the module tray on a sunny windowsill inside; from early summer move it outside.

How? Almost fill the module cells with compost and tap the tray on the table gently to settle the compost. Place in a sink of water until the surface is moist or water from above with a watering can, then leave for a few minutes to drain. Sow two lettuce seeds on the surface of each module, then barely cover with more compost.

What next? When the seedlings are big enough to handle, remove the weaker one. Then, when your seedlings have five leaves, transplant them either to larger containers or garden soil, at a spacing of about 30 cm (12 in). Harvest them before they bolt (get leggy and sprout upwards as if trying to take off), when the leaves will start tasting bitter.

Where have I gone wrong? Watch out for slugs and snails (*see page 36*), downy mildew and botrytis. *See Edible Garden Enemies, page 134.*

Weekend Project: The Impatient Salad Box

Here's one for the itchy-fingered. Sow these fast-growing crops in a window box from mid spring and you'll have the earliest harvest possible. Pop them on a sunny, sheltered window ledge outside for a peppy, crunchy salad for the new season.

YOU WILL NEED
1 window box with drainage holes
multipurpose compost
1 packet of radish seed such as 'French Breakfast'
1 packet of rocket (arugula) seed
1 packet of mixed lettuce seed
30 minutes

Add a layer of crocks to the bottom of the box and fill almost to the top with compost. Roughly dividing the box into three portions, thinly sprinkle the radish, rocket (arugula) and lettuce seed onto the compost. Cover with a thin layer of compost, water well and place on a sunny, sheltered windowsill. Keep moist.

When the seedlings emerge, thin the radishes to 3 cm (1 in) apart. Harvest by cutting the rocket (arugula) and lettuce leaves above the smallest new leaf, and the radishes by pulling them up when they are big enough to eat.

Herbs

Herbs come from hot, dry countries so are great for the distracted, busy and forgetful gardener because they thrive on neglect. If you don't water them, they probably won't even notice.

I like having herbs in the garden because it makes me feel like I can cook. It saves you having to rush to the supermarket every time a recipe calls for a bunch of parsley or a few sprigs of thyme, buying packets you'll use half of and then leave in the fridge to turn to black slime (or maybe that's just me). I used to just buy those supermarket herbs in pots, but couldn't seem to keep them alive more than a couple of weeks, so now I either sow seeds or buy plants. Lots of herbs, such as rosemary, mint, thyme and sage, last for years so only need planting the once.

They're also some of the best-looking plants in the garden and smell gorgeous. A row of weathered terracotta pots containing rosemary, basil and thyme looks the picture of elegance. Pop them by the back door and you won't even need to get your feet wet.

Here are some of the best-looking, best-tasting herbs to grow in a small space…

Basil

Basil can be sown direct into the containers you want to grow it in. Sow thinly and cover with a thin layer of compost in pots in mid-spring inside on a sunny windowsill. Alternatively, buy plants in spring/summer. When the basil germinates, keep it moist, but try not to water it in the evenings because basil hates going to bed with wet feet. When all fear of frosts is over, put your basil outside in a sunny, sheltered position.

When the plant gets bigger pinch out (and eat) the growing tips to encourage it to bush out. Pinch out the flowers when they appear. 'Sweet Genovese' is the one to choose for Italian-style mozzarella and tomato salads, pesto *(see Home-grown Pesto Sauce, page 78)* and pasta sauces. Purple basil looks lush and gorgeous. For Thai cookery, choose Thai (Horapha) basil *(see Weekend Project: Thai for Two, page 87)*. At the end of the summer, you can keep the plant going for a month or so by bringing it inside.

Mint

This must-have herb is a real bully, colonizing any bed you put it in. The traditional advice is to plant it in submerged pots in garden border to stop it taking over, but I tried this and the beast escaped within a season. So it's probably best in a fairly large pot. Mint is quite tolerant of shade, so is good for that tricky dark spot. It'll die down over winter but come back every year.

Where to start with varieties? For mint sauce, choose spearmint (traditional garden mint, Mentha spicata), Moroccan mint or apple mint. For mint tea, go for Eastern (desert) mint or Moroccan mint *(see Weekend Project: Herbal Tea for Three, page 33)*. For Mojito cocktails *(see A Mojito to Banish a Bad Day at the Office, page 130)* use spearmint. For the truly fancy, there's lime mint, orange mint, pineapple mint or chocolate peppermint, which tastes like chocolate mint wafers. A few leaves with freshly picked strawberries are the business.

Coriander (Cilantro)

Leafy and lush, coriander (cilantro) can be sown in medium-sized pots from early spring on a sunny windowsill inside or sown direct into the soil from mid spring to midsummer in a sunny or partially shady spot. Sow thinly on the surface of multipurpose compost and barely cover. Or buy plants in spring/summer. When buying seed or plants, make sure you buy a variety that is suitable for leaf rather than seed production. Coriander (cilantro) won't resprout once harvested, so you'll need to sow more than once to have a good supply throughout summer.

Parsley

Parsley can be very slow and fiddly to germinate so it's easier to buy plants that are readily available from mid-spring to summer. Choose from curly or French plain leaved and plant in a sunny or partially shaded position in moist soil. Parsley is very happy in containers and a row of the curly sort looks great as an edging. The curly sort is fantastically hardy over winter.

Chives

Either buy plants or sow a patch 1 cm (½ in) deep outside in containers or garden soil in a sunny or partially shaded spot from late spring. To harvest, snip leaves with scissors to within 3 cm (1 in) of the soil level. The lovely edible, pink pom-pom flowers look good on top of salads. It will die down in winter but should return year after year. Try digging up a portion in the autumn, potting it up and placing on a sunny windowsill to have fresh chives throughout winter *(see Bring in the heat lovers, page 107)*.

Rosemary

Buy plants in spring and plant in a sunny, well-drained position. Rosemary hates being waterlogged, so if your soil is prone to being claggy, dig in some grit, shingle or sharp sand. It does well in pots. Pick leaves as and when you want them – delicious added to the roasting tin with baby salad potatoes and garlic or with lamb.

Thyme

Thyme is fairly easy to grow from seed, but takes a while to get going, so it's easier to buy plants. There are some gorgeous varieties out there, from common

Are potted supermarket herbs a no-no?

We've all bought those little pots of parsley, basil or coriander (cilantro), popped them on the kitchen windowsill and then watched as they flop over and die. This happens because the plants have been sown too close together and raised in hothouse conditions that encourage sappy, overcrowded growth. In order to get any decent life out of these plants, therefore, they should be cut back to encourage new growth and then divided carefully and potted up into, say, five separate pots. Sounds too much like hard work to me, especially when it's so easy to grow your own from seed or buy decently raised plants from garden centres.

(garden) thyme *(Thymus vulgaris)* to deliciously scented lemon thyme and the variegated 'Silver Queen'. Thyme hates being waterlogged so plant in a sunny, well-drained spot in garden soil. It's happy in containers – a simple planting of thyme in a good terracotta pot with a mulch of shingle looks lovely. Snip leaves as and when you want them, adding them to stocks, soups, marinades and stews. After flowering, trim the plant into a tidy shape to stop it becoming leggy.

Sage

Low-maintenance, handsome and evergreen, sage looks good all year round. Fry in butter and add to pasta with Parmesan for a fantastically easy supper. Buy plants in spring or summer and plant in a sunny, well-drained spot or pot. They'll be trailing over the edge in no time. Plants last several years. Purple sage is particularly pretty, though a bit wimpy compared to the green sort.

Bay

A bay tree in a nice terracotta pot is really elegant on a terrace or balcony. Bay is evergreen so looks good all year round and, because you only ever use one or two leaves at a time, you'll never exhaust the plant. Either leave plants to grow as bushes or prune off the sideshoots to make a posh lollipop shape worthy of a classy Italian trattoria.

Lemon verbena

The scent of this herb is my favourite smell in all the world. It also makes the best herbal tea. Buy a plant in spring, plant in a pot and put it in a sunny, sheltered position. Simply pull off five or six leaves and pour boiling water over for a lovely refreshing tea *(see Weekend Project: Herbal Tea for Three, page 33)*. After flowering, snip back the branches to a growing bud to stop the plant becoming too leggy and in winter bring it inside to a cool, light room and reduce watering to a minimum.

Oregano

Is oregano the same as marjoram? I'm never quite sure. They taste the same to me. This mainstay of Italian and Greek cookery is great in tomato sauces, with roast meats and on pizzas. It's best to buy in plants and plant them in a sunny, well-drained spot in containers or garden soil. The green varieties are pretty enough, but there are also gorgeous variegated or golden varieties. Trim back in the autumn to keep

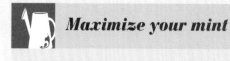

Maximize your mint

Give mint a haircut in midsummer when it's starting to look a bit coarse, cutting the stems back halfway to just above a bud. It will produce lovely, delicate new leaves for autumn. And, if you want fresh leaves throughout winter, dig up a portion of root in autumn, put it in a pot with fresh compost and place on a sunny windowsill (*see Bring in the heat lovers, page 107*). You could be fighting your hangover with a fresh mint tea on New Year's Day.

plants tidy. They die down a bit in winter, although in mild areas you could still be picking leaves in the coldest months.

Sorrel

Intensely lemony, this little salad herb is great for adding a fresh tang to salads and also makes a sublime early spring soup. It's perennial so once established, it'll keep coming back with no work from you and it's one of the earliest plants in the garden to make its appearance. It doesn't mind a shady spot either. Sow from early spring to early autumn, or buy plants from mid-spring. Buckler leaf or French sorrel is best for salads, Broad-leaved for soup. Or tr blood-veined sorrel if you're feeling flash.

THE ANISEEDY ONES...

Tarragon

Delicious in a mayonnaise for a chicken salad, this subtly flavoured plant has pretty, narrow leaves. It's not hardy in the cold so needs to be brought inside in the autumn. Buy plants, making sure you get French tarragon rather than the much less subtle Russian tarragon.

Fennel

With its delicate ferny leaves and impressive height fennel strikes a dramatic pose in any edible garden. Herb (common) fennel (Foeniculum vulgare) is an easier plant to grow and rises up to almost 2 m (6 ½ ft) so is great in the centre of a bed. The stunning bronze form is a garden designer's dream. For how to grow Florence fennel, with its succulent white bulb, *see Summer Jobs, page 88*.

Chervil

A feathery herb that tastes really good with broad (fava) beans. Buy plants or sow in pots or garden soil from late spring. It's also very hardy so another sowing in early autumn will keep you in leaves throughout winter (*see page 102*). See also *Herb Butter, page 92 and Freeze some herbs, page 97*.

Weekend Project: Herbal Tea for Three

I love making herbal tea from herbs in the garden. There's something so wonderfully simple about picking a few leaves, popping them in a cup and covering with boiling water. It makes you feel all Zen, like the sort of person who can do the Downward Dog in yoga without crying.

You will need
3 medium-sized pots with drainage holes, at least 20 cm (8 in) in diameter
multipurpose compost
1 camomile plant – use Roman chamomile (Chamaemelum nobile)
1 lemon verbena plant
1 mint plant –
any will make a nice cup of tea, but the following make the tastiest: spearmint (garden mint), Moroccan mint, Eastern (desert) mint, black peppermint
45 minutes

Add a layer of crocks to the bottom of the pots and then fill them almost halfway with compost. Make a small hollow in the centre of the compost and plant one herb in each pot. Firm in with more compost and water well. Place in a sunny spot.
Camomile tea is supposed to help fight a cold. It's also meant to have a calming effect so is one to drink before bed. Put three or four fresh camomile flowers at the bottom of a cup and cover with boiling water for five minutes. Mint helps the digestion so is good after a big meal or night out – put four or five leaves in a cup and pour over boiling water. And there is no better way to end a good al fresco supper on a warm summer's evening than lemon verbena tea (*see page 32*). It helps the digestion, has mild sedative properties and an incredible zingy, lemon-sherbet scent.

Tomatoes

DIFFICULTY RATING

If I could only grow one thing in my garden, it would be tomatoes. It's a no brainer. I know people always say that home-grown vegetables taste better, but in the case of tomatoes, they really do. However good the shop-bought vine tomatoes now are – and unmistakable strides have been made since those scarlet ping-pong balls of my childhood – none can compare with a home-grown tomato, warmed by the sun. They smell lovely, they look great and they taste out of this world.

I stick to cherry varieties since I find these easiest to grow outside. The perennial old reliables 'Gardener's Delight' and 'Sungold' have never let me down. The golden-coloured Sungolds, particularly, rarely make it into the house. A salad of Sungolds mixed up with red cherry tomatoes looks and tastes fantastic. But you could also try baby plum tomatoes such as 'Santa', the red-and-yellow striped 'Tigerella' or impress discerning friends with 'Black Krim', a Russian beefsteak tomato with a purple blush.

Upright or cordon types grow straight upwards and look great tied to wigwams or fences, their fruits arching out on trusses among the vivid green leaves. Bush or trailing types sprawl over the sides of pots or window boxes or trail down gorgeously from hanging baskets.

You can buy tomato plants at garden centres from late spring to midsummer. However, if you want to grow unusual varieties (such as 'Sungold' or 'Tigerella') or simply like the idea of growing your own from scratch, then sow them on a sunny windowsill in mid-spring.

Sowing tomatoes

When? Mid-spring

Where? Inside on a sunny windowsill

YOU WILL NEED

Several small pots (7.5 cm/3 in ones are ideal), multipurpose compost, tomato seeds, 20 minutes

How? Three-quarters fill your pots with compost and stand them in an inch or so of water (the kitchen sink is ideal) until the surface of the compost is damp. Remove from the water to drain for a few minutes. Place two seeds on the surface of the compost in each pot. Cover with a thin layer of compost.

What next? Over the next few days, don't let the compost dry out. After about a week, your tomato seedlings will emerge. Continue to keep the compost moist but not wet and turn the tray regularly so that the seedlings don't grow crooked towards the light. When the seedlings are about 3 cm (1 in) high, remove the weaker seedling in each pot. For planting out instructions, see *Planting out tomatoes, page 80.*

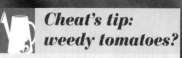

Cheat's tip: weedy tomatoes?

If your tomato seedlings start looking stretched and weedy, don't worry. Simply replant them in another pot so that the seed leaves (the bottom pair) are resting on the compost. New roots will soon grow from the buried stem.

EDIBLE GARDEN PUBLIC ENEMY NO. 1: SLUGS AND SNAILS

Life of slime...

You may think you like animals. You may even cry at ads for animal cruelty on cable channels on TV. Once you've sown your first seed, though, there's one group of animals you'd gladly see squirming in salt: slugs and snails.

These voracious destroyers of plant life will turn the most mild-mannered, live-and-let-live type to a blank-eyed assassin. They crawl out from their secret hiding places at night and lay waste to seedlings in a few hours. They bite cleanly through the stems of runner bean plants, make lettuces disappear overnight and cover your precious seedlings in slime, eating their tips so they rot and die. I don't consider myself particularly evil, but I've been known to cut slugs in half with secateurs and enjoy it.

Sentimentalists think they can just throw them over the garden fence. It doesn't work. I've heard of people dabbing Tipp-Ex onto snails' shells and throwing them as far away as they can, only to see those same Tipp-Exed snails reappearing in their garden the next evening. These creatures aren't stupid.

The best way to avoid slug and snail damage is to grow your crops in pots or high out of reach in hanging baskets or window boxes. They may be clever, but they haven't yet learned to fly. If you're growing crops in the soil you could try any one of the countless methods frequently attempted by the slug-desperate and snail-deranged.

How do you get rid of slugs and snails?

• **Melon or grapefruit skins.** Pop these out at night and in the morning you'll find a nice little colony of slugs and snails enjoying a light breakfast. You can then dispose of them in the bin. This seems OK, but there's only so much grapefruit you can eat.

• **Beer traps.** Plastic traps you fill with beer. Come morning you find lots of drunk and dead slugs and snails that you tip into the bin. Not bad, but you won't catch them all this way.

• **Ground egg shells.** Utterly useless in my opinion.

• **Coffee grounds.** Ditto.

• **Snail and slug pellets.** Effective, but evil. For the truly desperate, there are those little blue pellets of death containing metaldehyde that can be sprinkled around everything in a sort of assassin's ring. This might work, but is also the least environmental option, and even though I hate slugs and snails I'm rather fond of my toddler who runs around the garden putting random things in his mouth. You can get organic, less harmful versions of pellets, though (look for those based on aluminium sulphate and ferric phosphate). These are worth trying.

• **Nematodes.** These are microscopic natural predators that kill slugs for you. The slug nematode (Phasmarhabditis hermaphrodita) is a teeny eelworm that releases bacteria into slugs, which kills them. Nemaslug comes as a beige powder that you mix up in a watering can and sprinkle onto the soil. There's something undeniably satisfying about unleashing a righteous army of soldiers, even if they are invisible to the naked eye. This only kills slugs, however.

• Nightly trips outside with a torch and a large bowl of hot or salty water, cheap red wine or beer. (Cold tap water doesn't work because the wily things will just crawl out.) It may not quite fit in with your social schedule, but, honestly this really gets rid of any snail problem. Start in spring when your plants are tiny and at their most vulnerable. Simply pop the little horrors into the bowl so they drown. The first night, you'll catch 30, maybe 40. The second, the same again. But then you'll start noticing the numbers fall. All go into my red wine to die what I like to think is a convivial death, in a little cocktail party of doom.

Salad potatoes

DIFFICULTY RATING

Jargon buster: chitting potatoes

The world of potato growing seems to be riven with more jargon than that of any other vegetable. 'Seed potatoes' are just potatoes you buy and plant to get more potatoes. If someone tells you they've been 'chitting' in the greenhouse, don't call social services, they're merely placing their seed potatoes in a light place – windowsills are perfect – so that they can develop shoots so they get off to a head start. Potatoes are placed 'rose end up' – so that the end with the beginnings of new shoots points up. People often use egg boxes for this, though don't feel you need to suddenly get through a dozen Columbian Blacktail eggs – any container that holds them upright will do. Leave them there for two or three weeks until the shoots or 'chits' are a couple of centimetres long. Then they're ready for planting.

Home-grown salad or new potatoes taste better than the ones in the shops. They just do. They're fresher, earthier and you can choose from some wonderful varieties. Above all, there's something very satisfying about upturning a bucket of potato plants on the patio and seeing the perfect spud treasure roll out to be made into a delicious salad there and then.

I only ever grow potatoes in containers since they grow so well this way. I also only grow salad potatoes because the large ones for baking, mashing and roasting are so cheap and take so long to grow. Buy any first or second early potato variety from a garden centre or online specialist. My favourites are 'Mimi', which are tiny with red skins, the classic salad spud 'Charlotte', nutty 'Anya' and buttery 'Harlequin'. For a really early harvest, go for 'Swift' or 'Rocket'. This year I'm having a go at growing the blue 'Vitolette', a French salad spud that is dark blue from its skin all the way through and tastes like buttery chestnuts. Eat your freshly dug spuds hot with butter, cold with mayonnaise or in a warm salad with feta, chives and baby beetroot (beet). Glorious.

Planting potatoes

When? Start by laying them out for chitting (*see above*) on a light windowsill in early spring. By mid-spring they are ready for planting out.

YOU WILL NEED

A container with drainage holes, multipurpose compost, seed potatoes (preferably chitted, though this is not essential), 20 minutes

---

Where? In any medium to large container (at least 25 cm diameter). You can use normal terracotta or plastic pots, or buy specially designed plastic potato barrels with lift-uppable sides. Growing salad potatoes in pots is really popular and there are loads of ingenious containers now available designed to look good and be easily movable. Some are bags made of thick-woven fabric, transformed into rustic loveliness by woven willow surrounds. For sheer ease, you can't really beat 'Spud Tubs', simple black plastic pots that are light to move around and have a certain minimalist appeal. They're perfect for those gardening on a balcony or terrace because you can roll them up and put them away when you're not using them. Pop three tubers in each.

How? Put a layer of crocks in the bottom of the container. Fill with 15 cm (6 in) of multipurpose compost and then place your potatoes on top of it with their chitted sprouts upwards. A 30 cm (12 in) diameter pot would take two potatoes. Adjust the quantity of potatoes depending on how big your pot is. Cover with another 15 cm (6 in) layer of compost. Water well. Place the container in a sheltered spot.

Mulch ado...

Many established crops such as strawberries, blueberries, raspberries, blackberries, figs and peaches could do with a mulch of garden compost or well-rotted manure in early spring. It helps keep moisture around the roots and provides nutrients to encourage healthy new fruits to grow. If you have an established compost bin, just chuck a few garden forkfuls of well-rotted stuff around the base of the plants or tree. If your compost has yet to rot down, it's worth buying a few bags of well-rotted manure or mushroom compost from a garden centre instead.

What next? When the shoots start to poke up through the compost add enough compost to cover them. If frost is forecast, cover the shoots with newspaper or fleece. Keep adding compost as the sprouts poke up and keep it all well watered. Eventually, the shoots will reach to the top of the pot and you'll have no more room to add compost. At this stage, start giving the pot a fortnightly feed of tomato feed or liquid seaweed.

When will they be ready? It depends on the variety. Generally, first earlies take about ten weeks and second earlies about 13 weeks. Have a rummage around to check how they're getting on before impatiently upturning the whole pot. I can't count the number of times I've found garlic-clove-sized potatoes where proper-sized ones should be. It's worth pulling out just as many potatoes as you need for supper so the others can continue to grow.

Where have I gone wrong? The fungal disease blight is the main potential foe of potatoes, though it's unlikely to be a problem with salad potatoes. Other less serious problems may include common scab. *See Edible Garden Enemies, page 134.*

Sugar snap peas and mangetout (snow peas)

DIFFICULTY RATING

If you have an acre of kitchen garden and a legion of gardeners, by all means sow row upon row of regular peas and enjoy freshly podded peas all summer long. If, like me, you have a small garden/patio, this isn't going to work. Peas take up space, they need supports and they're fiddly to shell. And when you can buy cheap, delicious frozen ones that were ushered into the freezer within minutes of being picked, I really don't see the point.

But I do make an exception for sugar snaps and mangetouts (snow peas). You get to eat the whole pea, after all, and their sweetness and crunchiness when just picked are eye-opening. Eaten raw in salads or briefly stir-fried to tender but crunchy with a little garlic and ginger, they are exquisite. Try growing them in a hanging basket, a growing bag or container, or in garden soil. For an easy life, choose a dwarf variety and you won't have to provide much support for them to climb up. If you plant in a hanging basket they will trail down. Good varieties are 'Sugar Snap' for a tall sugar snap; 'Sugar Rae', 'Sugar Bon' or 'Zucolla' for a dwarf sugar snap; and 'Dwarf Sweet Green' or 'Norli' for a dwarf mangetout (snow pea). Or why grow green at all? Purple-podded peas are great eaten as mangetout (snow pea), and look fabulous planted among sweet peas.

Sowing sugar snap peas and mangetout (snow peas)

When? Late spring to early summer.

In pots

> **YOU WILL NEED**
>
> A container at least 45 cm (18 in) in diameter with drainage holes, multipurpose compost, pea sticks (such as old prunings, the twiggier the better) at least 40 cm (16 in) long, sugar snap pea or mangetout (snow pea) seeds (a dwarf or compact variety), 20 minutes

How? Add a layer of crocks to the bottom of the container and then fill it almost to the top with compost. Push a handful of pea sticks into the

Weekend Project: A Salad Box for Shade

Even a shady sill can be used to grow salad. In fact, some things positively prefer to be out of the sun. Blood-veined sorrel has beautiful dark green leaves etched with purple veins and adds a deliciously citrus tang to salads. The spiky chives behind with their purple pom-pom flowers and interspersing of red and green lettuce in front complete the picture.

You will need
1 large window box with drainage holes, at least 60 cm (2 ft) long
multipurpose compost
1 blood-veined sorrel plant (Rumex sanguineum) – if you can't find this, try the low-growing Bucker's Leaf or French Sorrel rather than the more leggy Broad-leaved sorrel
2 chive plants
3 green lettuce seedlings, such as 'Green Salad Bowl' or 'Lollo Biondi'
2 red lettuce seedlings, such as 'Red Salad Bowl' or 'Lollo Rossa'
45 minutes

Add a layer of crocks to the bottom of the container and then three-quarters fill it with compost. Plant the sorrel in the centre at the back and the chives either side. Then plant the lettuces, alternating in colour, along the front of the bed. Firm around the plants with more compost and then water well. Keep moist.
Either snip off individual leaves from the lettuces as and when you want them or wait until they are mature and harvest them whole.

compost, evenly spaced (unless you're planting in a hanging basket in which case no supports are needed). Push your seeds into the compost as far as the middle joint of your forefinger (about 5 cm/2 in) and about 5 cm (2 in) apart. Water well and place in a sunny or partially shaded spot.

In garden soil

YOU WILL NEED

Pea sticks at least 40 cm (16 in) long (even longer for tall varieties) or a wigwam or obelisk, sugar snap pea or mangetout (snow pea) seeds, 20 minutes

How? Choose a sunny or partially shaded spot with moist, well-cultivated soil. Spacing and depth of sowing as for pots, above. If sowing a dwarf variety, use pea sticks as support. If sowing a tall variety, either use extra-tall pea sticks or sow around the base of a wigwam or obelisk (you may need to provide extra support with string tied horizontally around the obelisk in the early stages).
What next? If you want a constant supply of peas over the summer, resow when your seedlings are about 5 cm (2 in) high. Keep the pea seedlings moist as they emerge. Snip off the pods and eat them whole about three months after sowing.
Where have I gone wrong? Powdery mildew is the main thing to look out for with peas *(see Edible Garden Enemies, page 134)*.

Give pea (tips) a chance

Why not sow a pot of peas just for shoots? The tips of pea plants are a wonderful curiosity and delicious raw in salads, combining an unmistakable pea flavour with a fresh crunch. They'll be ready far before the actual peas. Sow as above and, when the plants are about 15 cm (6 in) high, snip off the top pair of leaves at the top of their stems. They will resprout after a couple of weeks. Scatter the shoots on the top of salads and see how long it takes your guests to work out what they are *(see A Salad to Put Spring in Your Step, page 52)*.

Carrots

DIFFICULTY RATING

Juice them, dip them in hummus and tzatziki *(see The Very Freshest Tzatziki, page 128)*, make cakes out of them, or just pull them up and eat them after washing the soil off under the garden tap. Carrots are to be filed in that category of vegetables you thought you didn't rate that much until you grew them yourself. It's something to do with the sugar, no doubt, that turns to starch soon after picking. A freshly picked one really does have the edge on a shop-bought variety, with a sweetness that is addictive, particularly if you grow the tender, early varieties recommended below.

Grow them in the garden soil, in window boxes or pots. They're slow-growing, but harvest them small and you'll really get the benefit of their crisp sweetness. I sow a couple of big pots of them in early spring for sweet baby roots that we eat raw or lightly steamed.

Try 'Amsterdam Forcing', 'Early Nantes' or 'Sytan' or, if you want to try a yellow one, 'Yellowstone'. For pots or window boxes, the small round ones such as Paris Market or Parmex are a good choice or stubby, tapered Chantenay. Since carrot fly can be a problem, it's also worth considering 'Resistafly' and 'Flyaway', which have built-in resistance to this pest.

Sowing carrots

When? Mid-spring to midsummer

In pots

YOU WILL NEED

A medium to large container with drainage holes, multipurpose compost, carrot seeds, 20 minutes

How? Add a layer of crocks to the bottom of the container and then fill it almost to the top with compost. Sprinkle the carrot seeds thinly over the surface and barely cover with compost. Water well and place in a sunny, sheltered position.

In garden soil

YOU WILL NEED

A pencil or stick, carrot seeds, 10 minutes

How? Choose a sunny or partially shaded spot in well-cultivated soil that hasn't had manure or compost recently added (carrots don't like it). With your pencil or stick, scratch a shallow groove in the soil. Sprinkle the carrot seed thinly along it, then cover with soil and water well.

What next? When the seedlings are big enough to handle, thin them to about 5 cm (2 in) apart. Investigate how big the roots have become and pull them up when you like the look of them.

Where have I gone wrong? Carrot fly is the main pest *(see Edible Garden Enemies, page 134).*

Pak choi

DIFFICULTY RATING

Lush, leafy and with a satisfying crunch, pak choi is surprisingly easy to grow. You can either harvest it as baby leaves 30 days after sowing – it's lovely raw in salads – or let the plants mature and steam them or add to stir-fries and soups. Group a container of pak choi with pots of oriental herbs and chillis for the ultimate outdoor Eastern larder (*see Weekend Project: Thai for Two, page 87*). Sow again (or buy plants) in summer for leaves that will survive the coldest frosts (*see Pak choi for the cold months, page 96*). Good varieties include 'China Choi'; generally the green-stemmed cultivars are tastier than the white-stemmed ones.

Sowing pak choi

When? Late spring to late summer.

In pots

YOU WILL NEED

A large container with drainage holes, multipurpose compost, pak choi seeds, 20 minutes

How? Add a layer of crocks to the bottom of the container and then fill it almost to the top with compost. Sow thinly 2 cm (½ in) deep. Water. Place in a sunny or partially shaded spot.

In garden soil

YOU WILL NEED

A pencil or stick, pak choi seeds, 10 minutes

How? Choose a sunny or partially shaded spot with well-cultivated soil. With your pencil or stick, scratch a shallow groove in the soil. Sprinkle the pak choi seed along it (seed spacing as above), then cover with soil and water well.

What next? For baby leaves, thin to about 8 cm (3 in) when seedlings are big enough to handle. Cut baby leaves after about 30 days, snipping above the smallest new leaf – the plant should resprout a couple of times. For mature plants, thin to 15 cm (6 in) apart. Leave plants to mature if you want bigger leaves to steam or stir-fry.

Where have I gone wrong? Pak choi can suffer from flea beetle, aphids, caterpillars, root fly *(see Edible Garden Enemies, page 134)* and slugs and snails *(see page 36)*.

Beetroot (Beet)

DIFFICULTY RATING

Banish all thoughts of the brutal vinegar-soaked purple wedges of your childhood. Home-grown beetroot (beet), harvested small, roasted and added whole to a warm late-spring salad is a different thing altogether – gorgeously sweet and aromatic. Or leave them until summer and slice them to show off their vivid hearts. Sow 'Pablo', 'Pronto', 'Bull's Blood' for a deep red one with the bonus of striking red leaves or 'Burpee's Golden' for golden yellow. My favourite, though, is 'Chioggia', which, when sliced, reveals perfect concentric rings of red and white that make salads look a bit special. I like growing them in medium-sized pots, or they look just as good in rows or clumps in the border.

Sowing beetroot (beet)

When? Early spring in modules inside, mid-spring to midsummer outside.

In modules

YOU WILL NEED

A module tray, multipurpose compost, beetroot (beet) seeds, 20 minutes

How? Almost fill the module cells with compost. Water and leave to drain. Sow four seeds per cell, covering with 1 cm of compost. Place on a sunny windowsill inside.

What next? Keep moist. When the seedlings are 5 cm (2 in) high, plant out in garden soil or pots outside, allowing 10 cm (4 in) between each cell.

In pots

YOU WILL NEED

A medium-sized container with drainage holes, multipurpose compost, beetroot (beet) seeds, 20 minutes

How? Add a layer of crocks to the bottom of the container and then fill it almost to the top with compost. Sprinkle your seeds thinly over the surface, then cover with a thin layer of compost. Water. Place in a sunny or partially shaded spot.

In garden soil

YOU WILL NEED

A pencil or stick, beetroot (beet) seeds, 10 minutes

How? Choose a sunny or partially shaded spot with well-cultivated soil. With your pencil or stick, scratch a shallow groove in the soil. Sow seeds about 5 cm (2 in) apart. Cover with soil and water well.

What next? Pull up the beetroots (beets) when they're golf-ball sized.

Where have I gone wrong? Watch for slugs and snails *(see page 36)*. Plants can 'bolt' (run to seed before growing a root) if they get too dry so keep them well watered.

Chard

Every allotmenteer grows it, veg box schemes are rarely without it and in farmers' markets you can't move for the stuff. Chard is certainly popular to grow, but what do you do with it and does anyone actually want to eat it? 'Looks pretty but I don't think anyone actually likes it,' said a friend when I mentioned it the other day.

It's true that chard isn't everyone's favourite. But if you like spinach, you'll probably like it. Why not just grow spinach then, you might wonder. Well, because spinach is hard to grow – it runs to seed at the slightest change in temperature and needs constant moisture around its roots. Chard, on the other hand, thrives on neglect, grows through a drought and would probably survive a brutal attack with a garden hoe.

Even those who don't admire chard's culinary virtues have to admit that it's a beautiful-looking plant, with lush, deep green leaves and Day-Glo midribs of pink, yellow or orange worthy of fluorescent highlighter pens. One plant will also last

for months. Cut the outer leaves as and when you want them and the plant will, triffid-like, keep on producing more. Cut the leaves when small for salads or steam big leaves and dot with melted butter and freshly ground black pepper.

For colour, go for 'Bright Lights' or Rainbow chard. Gourmets prefer the classic Swiss chard with thick, white stems. Sown again in late summer or early autumn a few plants dotted throughout the border are a very welcome sight in the lean times of winter.

Sowing chard

When? Early spring in modules inside, mid-spring-late-summer outside

In modules

 YOU WILL NEED

A module tray, multipurpose compost, chard seeds, 20 minutes

How? Almost fill the module cells with compost. Water and leave to drain. Sow one seed per cell, covering with 1cm (½ in) of compost. Place on a sunny windowsill inside.

What next? Keep moist. When the seedlings are 5 cm (2 in) high, plant out in garden soil or pots outside, allowing at least 20 cm (8 in) between them.

In pots

YOU WILL NEED

A medium to large container with drainage holes, multipurpose compost, chard seeds, 20 minutes

How? Add a layer of crocks to the bottom of the container and then fill it almost to the top with compost. Sow seeds 1 cm (½ in) deep about 10 cm

(4 in) apart. Cover with compost, water well and place in a sunny, sheltered spot. When the seedlings are big enough to handle, thin them to 20 cm (8 in) apart. Allow three plants to a 30 cm (12 in) diameter pot.

In garden soil

YOU WILL NEED

A pencil or stick, chard seeds, 10 minutes

How? Choose a sunny or partially shaded spot with well cultivated soil. Make 1 cm (½ in) deep holes with your pencil or stick about 30 cm (12 in) apart. Pop one seed in each hole, then cover with soil and water well.

What next? Keep the plants well watered. Pick off the outside leaves as and when you want them for cooking, or pick them when they're small and eat raw in salads.

Where have I gone wrong? Watch young plants for slugs and snails *(see page 36)*.

Cheat's tip: strawberry fast food

The usual time to plant strawberries is summer, but if you didn't do it last year, don't worry. You can buy and plant them now (*see Little Green Book, page 140 for suppliers*). These plants have been held in cold storage and, when planted in the spring, will bear fruit 2–3 months later – just about as near in the fruit world as you'll ever get to a ready-meal to go. If you planted strawberries last autumn, they should be flowering by now. When little fruits start to form, feed plants in containers with a liquid tomato or seeweed feed every fortnight.

Sweetcorn

Freshly picked, home-grown sweetcorn is the supermodel of the edible gardening world. The ultimate in growing-your-own showing off is ripping cobs off the plant and throwing them straight on the barbie (*see page 126*).

When picked and eaten quickly before the sugars have had time to turn to starch, sweetcorn is inestimably delicious. Unfortunately, there is a slight catch. Like a supermodel, sweetcorn is high-maintenance, demanding and prone to throwing huffs. It needs a sunny site in deep soil (so not one for containers) in order to develop decent-sized, ripe corn cobs. It needs to be planted close together. Most of all, though, it needs a long, hot summer.

But if you pull it off, the rewards are enormous. Not only do you get a taste to die for, but the plants bring a certain exotic flavour to the garden, with their lofty stems, dangly tassels on top and bulging cobs with their silks bursting out from the ends. Don't bother with those varieties called mini corn or baby corn, though. Even if they grow successfully, you'll only have enough for a small stir-fry.

Sowing sweetcorn

When? From mid-spring

Where? Inside on a sunny windowsill

YOU WILL NEED

7.5 cm (3 in) pots, multipurpose compost, sweetcorn seeds, 20 minutes

How? Fill your pots almost to the top with compost and then push one sweetcorn seed into each pot to a depth of about 2 cm (½ in). Water.

What next? Keep the seedlings moist and plant them outside in garden soil in early summer. For planting out instructions, *see Planting out sweetcorn, page 92*.

EDIBLE GARDEN PUBLIC ENEMY NO. 2: CATS

'My cats are no trouble in my vegetable beds,' cat owners always boast. 'That's because they're too busy ruining mine,' you reply. Cats, those charming beasts, aren't stupid. They don't crap in their own back yard, but head over to the neighbours where they powder their feline faces at leisure and dig up precious seedlings in the process.

When I redesigned my little city garden, I thought I was making six stylish raised beds. Apparently, I made six handy litter trays, the must-see destination of the feline world. My rocket (arugula) was the first casualty, taking a direct hit from above that made the thought of a green salad distinctly unappealing. Since then, I've been close to tears on discovering a row of just emerged salad leaves strewn brutally all over the place, topped, charmingly by cat doo-doo as if to add insult to injury. I swear all the neighbourhood cats have been sent a memo informing them of a particularly des. res. public convenience chez nous. Spring is the real problem time for cats because of a double whammy: the garden tends to be fairly bare, with lots of patches of earth – cat-toilet heaven – and there are lots of vulnerable seedlings coming up just waiting for feline annihilation.

So how do you deter your feline friends? I've tried strewing citrus peel around (apparently they don't like the smell), but that didn't seem to work and made the garden look like a compost heap. Some people swear by ultrasonic scarers and lion poo, available from garden centres, which is supposed to frighten them. But, for me, there is only one real solution: sticks. Not to beat them with, but to lay across the beds, the twiggier the better. Holly branches are also good since no one – not even a cat – wants to squat over prickles. Keep any prunings from fruit bushes and trees and raspberry canes, the thornier the better, pick up sticks in the local park or use bamboo canes if you don't have anything else, and create a criss-cross tangle upon which no cat would dare to tread. And don't forget to cover pots, too. If that fails, get a water pistol.

For more Edible Garden Enemies, see also page 134.

Aubergines (Eggplants)

DIFFICULTY RATING

Let's not kid ourselves, if you live in a Northern European climate you're never going to be able to grow aubergines (eggplants) as easily as you could in the Mediterranean or Middle East. But that just means making sure you choose a variety that's been bred for your climate and that produces small fruits, as opposed to enormous things that won't ripen properly. These small aubergines (eggplants) are wonderfully tender in stews like ratatouille or as kebabs on a barbie with halloumi cheese and courgettes (zucchinis). Plant a 'baby' variety such as 'Ophelia' or 'Orlando' in a container and put it in the sunniest spot you can find. Buy plants in early summer if you'd rather not grow them from seed. See Weekend Project: Ratatouille Riot, page 88.

Sowing aubergines (eggplants)

When? Early- to mid-spring

Where? Inside on a sunny windowsill

YOU WILL NEED

7.5 cm (3 in) pots, multipurpose compost, aubergine (eggplant) seeds, 30 minutes

How? Three-quarters fill your pots with compost. Place two seeds on the surface of the compost in each pot. Cover with a thin layer of compost and water.

What next? When the seedlings are 3 cm (1 in) tall, remove the weaker one. Keep the seedlings in as light a spot as possible, turning the pots regularly to stop them growing crooked towards the light. Keep the compost moist but not waterlogged. For planting out instructions, *see Planting out aubergines (eggplants), sweet peppers and chillis, page 84.*

Where have I gone wrong? Watch for aphids *(see Edible Garden Enemies, page 134).*

A Salad to Put Spring in Your Step

This simple salad makes the best of the first spring salad and vegetables ready in the edible garden. It's a celebration of the beginning of the growing season: baby broad (fava) beans, pea shoots, baby beetroot (beet) and tiny new potatoes may be small, but they're full of the sweetness and intense tastes of the new season.

Serves 3
8 or more small beetroot (beet)
20 or more baby new potatoes
3 handfuls of baby broad (fava) beans, podded
4 good handfuls of salad leaves
200 g (7 oz) feta cheese, cubed
2 salad onions (scallions), roughly chopped
1 good handful of pea shoots
salad dressing

Wash the beetroot (beet) and twist off their tops, then roast in a medium oven for about half an hour or until they are soft when pierced with a knife. Alternatively, boil them until tender. Leave to cool. Wash the potatoes and then boil or steam them until cooked. Steam the broad (fava) beans for a couple of minutes and then peel them – they should pop out of their jackets easily. When the beetroot (beet) are cool, rub off the skins and cut them into quarters.

Wash and dry the salad leaves and place in a large bowl along with the feta, beetroot (beet), broad (fava) beans, onions and potatoes. Top with the pea shoots. Drizzle with salad dressing and toss well before serving with warm crusty bread, ideally while the potatoes are still warm.

Courgettes (Zucchinis)

DIFFICULTY RATING

I love the huge, lush, sandpapery leaves, the cheerful, blousy, yellow flowers – apparently delicious deep-fried and stuffed with ricotta if you're feeling confident with a deep-fat fryer – and the way the little fruits seem to appear overnight. In a soup with chicken stock, rice and lemon zest or just sliced lengthways and griddled with olive oil and a spritz of lemon juice, they are damn fine.

Courgettes (zucchinis) come in two types: bushes and climbers. With their prolific flowers and eye-catching fruits, climbing varieties looks gorgeous clambering over an obelisk, arch or pergola, or up a trellis. Try 'Black Forest' or the wonderful 'Tromboncino' with its extraordinary long snake-like fruits that, if left to mature like a squash, are delicious. Bush types work better in pots or sprawling over a garden bed. 'Defender' is a good reliable variety, as is 'Tuscany', which is compact so particularly good for containers. But for something unusual try the round 'Eight Ball', yellow 'Gold Rush' or 'Soleil', or a stripy courgette (zucchini) such as 'Romanesco'.

Sowing courgettes (zucchinis)

When? Mid-spring

Where? Inside on a sunny windowsill

YOU WILL NEED

7.5 cm (3 in) pots, multipurpose compost, courgette (zucchini) seeds, 20 minutes

How? Fill your pots almost to the top with compost. Push one seed, on its side, 3 cm (1 in) deep into each pot and cover with compost. Water well.

What next? Keep moist. When roots start to show through the bottom of the pot, transplant each courgette (zucchni) plant into a larger pot. For planting out instructions, *see Planting out courgettes (zucchinis), page 90.*

Whole books are published on the subject of how to cope with the enormous surplus of courgettes (zucchinis) that you will apparently produce from your home-grown plants. This can give you the impression that you've failed if your plant isn't producing enough to run a small farm shop on a daily basis. Certainly, my plants have never read these books because they only seem to produce enough for a couple of people. Which is best, really, because I'm not too keen on courgette (zucchini) chutney.

Figs

DIFFICULTY RATING

Typical conversation around a fig tree on a terrace somewhere in northern Europe:

'Have you actually ever eaten any figs off your fig tree?'
'Of course I have.'
'How many?'
'Loads. At least ten.'
'And you've had it for, what, three years?'
Shrug.

It's lucky they look so gorgeous and exotic. It's also fortunate that, when you brush against them, their hand-shaped leaves release the heady, escapist scent of the subtropics. Lucky, because, when it comes to actually producing figs you can eat, these trees can be a little reluctant. Not when grown in a Mediterranean climate, of course – here they sprout out of church walls with reckless abandon. But if you live in a country where you can't rely on a long, hot summer and have winters that regularly dip below freezing, a fig tree might be best approached as a lovely ornamental with fruit bonuses rather than a reliable producer of pudding.

Having said that, a fig tree planted in a terracotta pot is a lovely thing, bringing a touch of glamour and exoticism to any garden, patio or balcony. There are also things you can do to increase its productivity, so if you're prepared to put a bit of effort in you will be rewarded.

The first thing is to choose a variety suited to your climate. 'Brown Turkey' is a popular choice with dark-red-fleshed fruits, although 'Brunswick' and 'Violetta' (which is particularly frost-resistant) are also good. Next, you need to restrict the roots by planting it in a container. This constrains the growth of the tree, which encourages fruit to form. Place the pot in a sunny, sheltered spot.

To have the very best chance of getting fruit, you also need to provide protection during winter. This is because the next year's figs start off in the autumn as little buds and these are liable to die if subjected to very cold temperatures. Either bring your fig tree into a light, cool place such as a porch or conservatory before the first frosts or – less hassle – cover with horticultural fleece (*see Jargon buster: horticultural fleece, page 118*). You can buy rather natty fleece 'jackets' from many garden equipment suppliers, which are basically fleece hoods with drawstrings that you can place over your tree, keeping the whole thing snug. You remove these in spring when frosts are over.

Finally, it's a good idea to pinch back the growing shoots in early summer to divert the tree's energies into fruit production rather than putting out long branches (*see Give a fig about pruning, page 88*).

If all that hasn't put you off, then you're in for a wonderful treat. Growing fig trees is a challenge, but the rewards, when they do come (and they do, I promise), are truly worth it: sweet, fragrant, meltingly soft fruits eaten straight off the tree.

Planting fig trees

When? Mid-spring to late summer
Where? Outside in a pot

YOU WILL NEED

A container at least 45 cm (18 in) in diameter, multipurpose compost, a fig tree, available from all garden centres or online fruit suppliers (specialist fruit suppliers will provide the biggest range), 30 minutes

How? Add a layer of crocks to the bottom of the container and then half fill it with compost. Carefully ease your fig tree out of its shop-grown pot and, with your fingers, tease out the roots a little if they look constricted. Then make a hole in the compost in the container and place the tree in it, covering with more compost so that the tree is planted at the same level it was before. Water in well and place in the sunniest, most sheltered position you can find.

What next? Keep the tree well watered and feed every couple of weeks with liquid seaweed. For further aftercare see page 88 and page 107.

Where have I gone wrong? Immature fruit dropping off could be a sign of inadequate watering – you may need to water every day in the height of summer.

Squashes and pumpkins

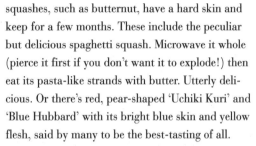

DIFFICULTY RATING

Dotted with orangey-yellow fruit and trailing around a terrace, a pumpkin or squash vine is the plant world's version of fairy lights. These are large, handsome plants, not to be confined. They like to sprawl, climb, trail and colonize. And, in return, they'll give you fiery-skinned squashes with nutty flesh just crying out to be roasted and swathed in melted butter, turned into mouthwatering soups or turned into handsome jack o'lanterns fit for Halloween.

The squashes split into two types. Summer squashes you eat straight off the plant in summer – such as the custard-yellow 'Sunburst'. Winter squashes, such as butternut, have a hard skin and keep for a few months. These include the peculiar but delicious spaghetti squash. Microwave it whole (pierce it first if you don't want it to explode!) then eat its pasta-like strands with butter. Utterly delicious. Or there's red, pear-shaped 'Uchiki Kuri' and 'Blue Hubbard' with its bright blue skin and yellow flesh, said by many to be the best-tasting of all.

If you're a pumpkin fan, choose 'Jack O'Lantern' for your perfect Halloween specimen, 'Rouge Vif d'E-tamps' for a giant fit for Cinderella's carriage and, for pots, the mini 'Baby Bear' – the seeds of which can also be toasted as a nice snack.

Sowing squashes and pumpkins

When? Mid-spring

Where? Inside on a sunny windowsill

YOU WILL NEED

7.5 cm (3 in) pots, multipurpose compost, squash or pumpkin seeds, 20 minutes

How? Fill your pots almost to the top with compost. Push two seeds, on their sides, 3 cm (1 in) deep into each pot. Cover with compost and water.

What next? When the seedlings are 3 cm (1 in) tall remove the weaker one. Keep moist. When roots start to show through the bottom of the pot, transplant each squash or pumpkin plant into a larger pot. For planting out instructions, *see Planting out squashes and pumpkins, page 91.*

Cucumbers

DIFFICULTY RATING

I thought I didn't like cucumbers much. They were watery, tasteless things, wrapped in plastic. But then I grew a few outdoor cucumber plants and I'm now a bona fide cucumber bore. The plants are pretty, climbing up a wigwam or obelisk with yellow flowers and lush green leaves, but it's the cucumbers themselves that are the real surprise. They have none of the wateriness of the shop-bought sort, and a far more satisfying, sweet flavour. Grow 'Burpless Tasty Green' or a miniature variety such as 'La Diva' up a wigwam. Or try the compact, non-climbing 'Bush Champion' if you're growing in a container. They make the perfect cucumber sandwich or grate them for amazing tzatziki *(see The Very Freshest Tzatziki, page 128)*.

Sowing cucumbers

When? Mid-spring

Where? Inside on a sunny windowsill

YOU WILL NEED

7.5 cm (3 in) pots, multipurpose compost, cucumber seeds, 20 minutes

How? Fill your pots almost to the top with compost. Push two seeds, on their sides, 3 cm (1 in) deep into each pot. Cover with compost and water.

What next? When the seedlings are 3 cm (1 in) tall, remove the weaker one. Keep moist. For planting out instructions, see *Planting out cucumbers, page 91.*

Weekend Project: A sweet way to banish a gloomy early spring day

In early spring, there are days the outside world looks so grey and barren all you want to do is get on a plane and escape the gloom. It's at times like this that I indulge in a little bit of comfort sweetpea sowing, aided and abetted by a large glass of wine and the cheesiest radio station I know, turned up high.

You will need
7.5 cm (3 in) pots
multipurpose compost
1 packet of sweet pea seeds
20 minutes

Fill the pots almost to the top with compost and then push three seeds into each pot to the depth of your middle finger joint. Cover with compost, water and place on a sunny windowsill, while singing along to a boy band you would never admit to liking in public.

Keep well watered to avoid powdery mildew *(see Edible Garden Enemies, page 134)*.

When the seedlings have emerged and have two sets of leaves, pinch out the growing points. This may seem ruthless, but it will make the plant much sturdier so it's well worth doing. Leave the seedlings to grow on until mid- to late spring and then plant them out at the foot of wigwams, obelisks or hazel twigs, up which they'll scramble like keen little mountaineers *(see Sweet companions, page 81)*.

Edible flowers

They're edible, not delicious. You wouldn't want a whole plate of these edible flowers, but as a garnish or sprinkled on top of a salad, they have a mild peppery taste and, more importantly, look absolutely gorgeous. They don't look half bad on the plant either.

Nasturtiums

Nasturtium flowers, with their upbeat bright yellow, orange or red tones, are as prolific as the plants they come from. You only need two or three plants and they'll sprawl heroically up obelisks and trellises and clamber in among other plants giving your garden a luscious air of colourful abandon and cottagey charm. My garden would be lost without them – they're great for covering bare earth and brightening up corners and love growing in containers as well as open ground. Choosing a form with variegated leaves gives them an even brighter look, or choose a dwarf form if you don't want it to clamber all over the place. Sow seed direct into garden soil in a sunny spot from late spring-early summer or in pots inside from mid-spring to get them off to an earlier start.

Or buy ready-grown plants, then stand back and wait for the colour explosion. Pick a handful and remove the stamens before throwing onto a mixed salad.

Borage

Borage is another plant perfect for the decorative edible garden. Its pretty, star-shaped blue flowers

taste a bit like cucumber and are a traditional addition to Pimm's (*see A Fruitful Pimm's, page 132*). They also look gorgeous suspended in an ice cube, or add them at the last minute to white wine and see the blue flower turn to pink. Either sow borage seed in mid-spring direct into garden soil in a sunny spot or buy a plant later in the season. It will sow itself once established so you only need to plant it once.

Viola tricolor (Heartsease)

Could any flower be cuter? Purple, mauve and a yellow blushing throat, all small enough to fit into the palm of your hand. Sow inside in mid-spring in 7.5 cm (3 in) pots on a sunny windowsill and then transplant outside to pots or garden soil when they're about 3 cm (1 in) tall to a sunny or partially shaded position. Alternatively, plants are readily available from garden centres. Buy a tray of plug plants and pack them into hanging baskets or containers. They'll flower right through autumn and winter if you regularly deadhead them. They look particularly nice growing among salad leaves (*see Weekend Project: A Salad Basket with Zing, page 69*).

Pot marigolds

Intense orange blooms and a reputation for attracting aphid-munching hoverflies have made pot marigolds (Calendula officinalis) a traditional kitchen garden favourite. They're also reputed to deter carrot fly (*see Edible Garden Enemies, page 134*) since their smell is supposed to confuse the pests. The vivid orange petals look pretty scattered on salads. Sow in late spring direct into garden soil in a sunny site or inside from early spring and transplant later.

FLOWERS TO INCLUDE JUST BECAUSE...

Yes, a lot of vegetables and fruit plants are pretty, but can they really compete with a forest of cosmea flowers waving in the breeze or a wall of clambering sweet peas? Not only will these flowers bring in pollinating insects such as bees, but just as

importantly, look gorgeous so you can lounge around with the Sunday papers, share a bottle of wine with a friend or just waft about and not feel you're in an allotment.

Obviously, the list of flowers you can grow in your garden is as long as you want it to be, but these are a good start, easy to start off from seed in early spring (or buy as plants later), cohabiting happily with fruit and veg, and reliably flowering through to late summer, in some cases even late autumn.

Sweet peas

If you're going to have one type of flower in your edible garden, better make it sweet peas. These delightful climbers have always grown cheek by jowl with vegetable and fruit plants. They're particularly good grown up the same wigwams as runner and French (green) beans since they flower magnificently from early summer before the beans establish themselves. Their sweet scent is famous and their variously coloured lobed flowers are wonderful for cutting and bringing into the house. I put them in vases on the outside table too. The more you cut, the more flowers you get.

My favourites are 'Dorothy Eckford' (white), 'Cupani Original' (purple and the most strongly scented), 'Painted Lady' (bi-coloured pale and darker pink) and 'Black Knight' with its wonderful crimson black. You can buy them easily as plants in late spring, though sowing them is no hassle and quite fun since it's something to do in the otherwise sparse days of early spring. For sowing instructions, see *Weekend Project: A sweet way to banish a gloomy early spring day, page 58.*

Cosmea

I adore these daisy-like flowers, held on high stems above ferny foliage. They form a jungle in my garden every year, poking out through butternut squashes or tomatoes, or lolling languidly over strawberry plants. They paper over the cracks of the kitchen garden, filling dead space and bringing a sense of joyful colour and abandon. I'd miss them if they weren't there.

A packet of Cosmos 'Sensation Mixed' will bring you flowers of white, light pink and dark pink from early June to the end of October. Sow, barely covering with compost, in 7.5 cm (3 in) pots on a sunny windowsill in mid-spring, two to a pot, and then thin to the strongest seedling when they are a couple of centimetres tall. Plant out into the garden or large pots in late spring when they are about 15 cm (6 in) tall. If they look leggy, pinch out the growing tip to encourage the sideshoots to bush out. Plant at least 30 cm (12 in) apart in a sunny spot in soil that has preferably had compost or well-rotted manure added. If planting in a pot, plant one to a 30 cm (12 in) diameter pot. Throughout the summer keep cutting off the dead flowers to encourage new blooms to grow.

Cheat's tip: stop weeding!

Annual flowers such as nasturtiums and cosmea freely self-seed, which means that seeds they drop at the end of the summer often germinate in the spring and pop up as brand new little plants. Don't pull them up; let them grow and save yourself the hassle of sowing new seed each spring.

Nicotiana sylvestris

These tobacco-plant giants bring a lush abundance to any garden, with their enormous sweet-smelling leaves and trumpets of white flowers that gradually appear over the summer until they're looming over all inferior species. The fragrance of the flowers, particularly at night, is intoxicating.

Carefully sow these tiny seeds in a module tray filled with compost on a sunny windowsill in early spring and then thin out to one plant per cell when the seedlings are big enough to handle. Transplant a seedling from its module cell to a 7.5 cm (3 in) pot when it swamps its module and then into open ground when it swamps its 7.5 cm (3 in) pot.

Californian poppies

So intensely, upliftingly orange, these are quite simply feel-good flowers. The odd clump dotted around the borders or in pots will trail beautifully and spread around, attracting admiring stares, bees and butterflies. Either sow direct into garden soil in late spring, or (more reliable in my experience) inside in a module tray or small pots in mid-spring and transplant later. They will self-sow once established.

Climbers

Planting a climber to scramble up your fence or wall is great in an edible garden. Not only do they add structure and colour year after year (most are perennial), but they bring in pollinating insects. The trellis fences of my tiny city garden play host to a white solanum, which flowers pretty much all year round, two honeysuckles, a jasmine, wisteria and two types of clematis. They soften the borders and, so long as they are pruned so they don't take over the space, cohabit happily with fruit and vegetable plants.

Tulips

Plant bulbs in autumn in pots or garden soil. A sea of pure white tulips looks gorgeous poking above a bed of salad crops.

Alliums

Try Allium christophii for a real firework of a flower, an enormous sherberty ball of star-shaped purple flowers on a tall stalk. Stunning. Plant bulbs in early autumn in pots or garden soil.

Dahlias

One of the most luscious flowers you can grow with blooms that come in all sorts of spectacular colours and shapes. My 'Bishop of Llandaff' with its deep crimson flowers and purplish leaves looks great when it gets into its stride in late summer. Plant tubers in spring or plants in summer. Traditionally, you're supposed to dig up the tubers and store them over winter, but I'm too lazy so leave them where they are, giving the plant a thick mulch of compost to protect the roots from frost in early winter. So far, it's come back every year.

Sweet peppers and chillis

A chilli or sweet pepper plant laden with green, orange and red peppers is gorgeously exotic and cheerful. So seductive are these plants that I grow chillis every year even though neither I nor anyone in my household has ever eaten anything spicier than a chicken korma.

If you enjoy burning your taste buds to oblivion, there's a dizzying range of chilli seeds out there to buy, from mild 'Hungarian Hot Wax', through Mexican 'Jalapeño' right up to the tiny but mighty hot Thai bird's eye chillis. I've had success with 'Etna', though have a browse online since new varieties are being introduced all the time.

In a northern European climate, they're best grown in containers so they can be moved inside in late summer for the chillis to fully ripen. They look great in brightly coloured pots or even metal fire buckets and also do well in large window boxes. Start them off in early-mid spring and you'll be eating them by early autumn. If you can't handle all those fresh chillis at once, dry them in a cool oven and then keep in an air-tight jar to crumble into curries, stir-fries and sauces whenever you feel the need. Just be sure to wash your hands before rubbing your eyes…

As for sweet peppers, plant them in a pot and choose the sunniest, most sheltered site possible for these hot-blooded creatures. They particularly like growing bags (three to a bag), where the fertilized compost provides them with lots of potash to encourage the growing fruits. But they'll also be happy in a large pot or window box where their large fruits look impressively exotic. All sweet peppers start green and then ripen through yellow and orange to red, getting sweeter the redder they are. The compact 'Redskin' and 'Antohi Romanian' are great for growing in pots. Or try 'Marconi Rosso' in growing bags for a tapered, long Italian variety. If you don't want to eat your sweet peppers green, you may need to bring the pot inside in the autumn to get them to fully ripen.

Sowing sweet peppers and chillis

When? Early-mid spring

Where? Inside on a sunny windowsill

YOU WILL NEED

7.5 cm (3 in) pots, multipurpose compost, chilli or sweet pepper seeds, 30 minutes

How? Three-quarters fill your pots with compost. Place two seeds on the surface of the compost in each pot. Cover with a thin layer of compost and water.

What next? When the seedlings are 3 cm (1 in) tall, remove the weaker one.

Keep the seedlings in as light a spot as possible, turning the pots regularly to stop them growing crooked towards the light. Keep the compost moist but not waterlogged. For planting out instructions, see *Planting out aubergines (eggplants), sweet peppers and chillis, page 84.*

Where have I gone wrong? Watch young plants for greenfly *(see Edible Garden Enemies, page 134)* and slugs and snails *(see page 36)*, which can make holes in the peppers.

Kale

DIFFICULTY RATING

I don't bother growing much of the brassica family, since they are, by and large, a magnet for pests and I don't want to cover my garden with anti-pigeon, anti-caterpillar netting and 24-hour surveillance cameras. I do, however, make an exception for kale, which I adore, not only for its hardiness, pest resistance and earthy, good-for-you taste, but also its wide variety of leaves and colours, from the frilly terracotta red of 'Redbor' to the almost black, crepe-like plume of leaves of black Tuscan kale (also known as 'Nero di Toscana' or Cavolo Nero)

that always reminds me of the Prince of Wales feathers. This is perhaps the hardiest one and my favourite. Others to recommend are the lush green 'Pentland Brig', 'Dwarf Green Curled' and 'Red Russian', which has prolific, crunchy, pink-ribbed leaves.

The thing I love most of all about kale, though, is that it exists at all. When your garden gets ready to shut down for winter, the kales aren't getting the message. I love them for that brazenness – the fact that they remind you that life hasn't just stopped. They just keep on growing through the darkest, shortest days and producing lush leaves that are delicious steamed with plenty of butter and black pepper. They're also wonderful in soups with chorizo *(see Kale and Chorizo Soup, page 25)* or borlotti beans. A winter roast isn't the same in our house these days without kale on the side. You'll be eating kale right up until mid-spring when the yellow flowers tower above the border, attracting pollinating bees to other flowers and crops around.

Sowing kale

When? Late spring

Where? On a sunny windowsill

YOU WILL NEED

A module tray, multipurpose compost, kale seeds, 20 minutes

How? Almost fill the module cells with compost and tap the tray down lightly on the table to settle the compost. Water from above with a watering can with a sprinkler attachment, then leave for a few minutes to drain. Sow one kale seed on the surface of each module and then cover with a thin layer of compost.

What next? Keep your seedlings moist when they emerge. For planting out instructions, *see Planting out kale, page 97.*

Summer

Sauntering barefoot around the garden before work, gathering a handful of blueberries and raspberries to add to muesli. The scent of freshly picked sun-warmed tomatoes. Nasturtium flowers crawling among the scarlet beads of runner bean blossoms. The smoky promise of a barbecue. It's summer, and in the edible garden it doesn't get much better than this. It's about long balmy evenings outside with friends, drinking Pimm's filled with freshly picked mint leaves and strawberries, munching bruschetta laden with your own heavenly tomatoes and basil. In short, it's about the sun, the company and, most of all, the food.

Early summer is still busy – time to plant tomatoes, beans, courgettes (zucchinis), cucumbers, aubergines (eggplants), sweetcorn and chillis. You can also continue sowing peas, beetroot (beet), salad and carrots. But later in the summer brings a welcome time of laziness in the garden. The activity of spring is long over. The garden's slow decline to winter is safely far away. Pretty much all there is to do is water, feed your plants and feed yourself. Popping outside for five minutes to pick courgettes (zucchinis), French (green) beans, strawberries and raspberries for supper – wafty hat and trug suitable, but not compulsory – certainly beats battling the supermarket aisles after work.

If you do only three things this season...

Plant tomatoes, plant strawberries, sow French or runner (green) beans

tomatoes

strawberries

French or runner (green) beans

Here comes the sun

Whether you have a garden or a couple of windowsills, the outside larder is at its fullest. You could be eating broad (fava) beans, carrots, French (green) beans, herbs, lettuces, courgettes (zucchinis), cucumbers, figs, tomatoes, chard, rocket (arugula), blueberries, peaches, plums, strawberries, raspberries, cherries, apricots, blackberries, garlic, beetroot (beet), herbs, sugar snap peas and towards the end, runner beans. It could also be a riot of colour out there – with cosmea, alliums, nasturtiums, dahlias and climbers flowering their little hearts out among your crops.

Oh, and you're going on holiday and leaving all your crops to wither on the plant…

How to go on holiday

Gardeners can't go on holiday. Ever. Or, at least, they can't unless they're prepared to come back to a garden they barely recognize. This is because, however nice your neighbours/extended family, no one will ever be able to water your precious garden like you can, let alone deadhead, tie in, prune and generally faff around your plants with all the attention of a penguin standing on its egg (admit it, you're obsessed). The universal crime committed by helpful holiday waterers is under-watering, particularly in containers. Bribe them with whole Camemberts, salamis, weekends in the Languedoc – anything to encourage them to water, and remind them before you go to particularly focus on window boxes, hanging baskets and pots. Remember: they need watering even when it rains. A potted plant in full leaf is a very effective umbrella.

Alternatively, if you don't have any helpful neighbours or are so obsessive that you wouldn't trust them even if you did, you could buy an automatic watering system with a timer (see *Little Green Book, page 140 for equipment suppliers*). These might sound horribly complicated, but are actually easy to set up and really take the hassle out of watering – whether your crops are in garden soil or pots – giving you the freedom to go away for the weekend or even long holidays without panicking about anything other than getting to the airport in time.

Weekend Project: A Salad Basket with Zing

This hanging basket looks adorable, with the contrast of the green and red salad leaves and spiky clumps of rocket (arugula), and the purple and yellow violas tumbling over the sides a sweet touch. Being up high, it'll be out of reach of slugs and snails.

You will need
1 plastic-lined hanging basket with drainage holes, at least 30 cm (12 in) in diameter
1 handful of water-retaining gel
multipurpose compost
3 'Green Salad Bowl' lettuce plug plants
3 'Red Salad Bowl' lettuce plug plants
5 Viola tricolor (Heartsease) plug plants
6 wild rocket (arugula) plug plants
30 minutes

Add a handful of water-retaining gel to the compost before planting to cut down on watering (*see Cheat's tip: hanging baskets, page 13*).
Fill the basket almost to the top with compost. Plant the lettuces, leaving a 6 cm (2.5 in) border clear around the edge. Then plant the viola and rocket (arugula) plug plants alternately around the edge. Firm in, water well and hang up in a sunny or partially shaded spot. Keep the compost moist. Just reach up with scissors and snip off your leaves as and when you want them, then add a sprinkling of peppery viola flowers to the top of your salad for the final touch. If you snip the lettuce and rocket (arugula) plants just above the smallest new leaf, they'll regrow several times.

Strawberries

An unfortunate, slug-related incident one summer left me with rather fewer strawberries than I had hoped for. This wouldn't normally matter, but I had some friends coming for lunch and had already bought the meringues and cream. I was forced to buy punnets of strawberries. From a shop. It felt bad.

Later I mixed in the few berries that had escaped attack and asked my friends if they could tell the difference. They all promised that my ones were somehow sweeter and better, but then, I was standing over them with a pruning saw.

There's something about growing your own strawberries that brings out the passionate in people. Maybe it's because they're the archetypal summer fruit. Or maybe it's because there's something a bit decadent and sensual about eating a sun-warmed strawberry straight off the plant. My theory is that it's something to

do with the seeds all being on the outside – there's nothing hard to watch out for in the middle.

You've got to have strawberries in your edible garden, however tiny it is. Even if you have only space for a hook on an outside wall, it's worth planting up a hanging basket. You can pick them at the peak of juicy ripeness, unlike the shop-bought ones, picked while

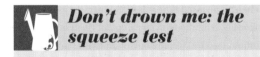

Don't drown me: the squeeze test

Strawberries will rot in sodden ground; a good test to see if you're overwatering is to squeeze a handful of compost. If water runs through your fingers, it's waterlogged. So lay off the watering for a while.

still firm enough for boxing up and putting on a lorry. Even a few plants can give you enough to smother in double cream, scatter on muesli or turn into a mouthwatering smoothie *(see Barefoot Breakfast Smoothie, page 72).*

The plants look cute, with scalloped leaves and daisy-like white and yellow flowers. I love the way the buttery, cushiony centre of the flower gradually swells into the fruit. They're adaptable, too, growing as well in open ground as they do in pots, window boxes and hanging baskets, where their fruits trail over the edges in a desultory way. A row of individual plants in small terracotta pots on a windowsill looks adorable. Or plant them at the front of a bed to make a cheerful, cottagey border.

Different varieties of strawberries are ready at different times so, to get fruit over a long period, it's a good idea to plant a spread of different ones. For example, 'Gariguette' or 'Alice' crop in early summer, 'Cambridge Late Pine' in midsummer and 'Chelsea Pensioner' in late summer. Many plant suppliers *(see Little Green Book, page 140)* sell helpful collections, which takes the hard work out of choosing. Alternatively, buy one of the 'ever-bearing' or 'perpetual' varieties, which will crop twice. These include 'Aromel', 'Viva Rosa' and 'Mara des Bois', which combines the delicious aromatic taste of a woodland strawberry with the size of a cultivated one.

And don't forget the alpine or woodland strawberry. They may be tiny, but just a couple placed on top of a pudding, for example, pack an intense taste way above their size and you certainly won't find them in the shops. *See also Cheat's tip: strawberry plants for free, above.*

Planting strawberries

When? The usual time is late summer, for a crop the following year, though you can plant them in early autumn too. You usually buy plants with bare, spider-like roots that need to be planted out straightaway before they dry out, though you'll also see potted plants for sale, which are fine too. Alternatively, plant cold-stored runners *(see Cheat's tip: strawberry fast food, page 48)* in spring for a fast crop you'll be eating by summer.

Cheat's tip: strawberry plants for free

Strawberry plants are terribly accommodating. They not only produce lots of luscious fruit, but also make it super easy to raise the next generation. By midsummer you'll notice your plants putting out 'runners', basically baby plants on the end of long stems. If you don't want extra plants, snip these long stems off close to the main plant. But if you do want to increase your number of strawberry plants next year, take a small pot and fill it with compost. Then place each baby plant, still attached to the runner, on top of the compost and tether it down with a piece of wire or pebble. After a couple of weeks, when the baby plant has rooted, you can snip it off. And, hey presto, you have a whole new plant that can be planted out in the ground in early autumn (space them about 30 cm/12 in apart) and which will give you a nice crop of fruit next summer.

In pots

YOU WILL NEED

A suitable container with drainage holes, multipurpose compost, strawberry plants, 45 minutes

How? Add a layer of crocks to the bottom of the container and then two-thirds fill it with compost. In window boxes and hanging baskets, it's a good idea to add a handful of water-retaining gel to the compost. Aim for three plants in a 30 cm (12 in) diameter hanging basket or pot, or up to six plants in a growing bag. If you're using a terracotta pocket planter, plant as many plants as you have pockets, but do put a good layer of crocks in the bottom because the lower plants tend to get waterlogged in these traditional-style pots.

In a window box, space them about 20 cm (8 in) apart. Spread out the roots of the plants and lay them on the surface of the compost so they are not squashed, then fill with more compost. Water well and place in a sunny or partially shaded spot. They're woodland plants so will be OK in light shade, though a sunny spot will result in sweeter berries.

In garden soil

> **YOU WILL NEED**
>
> Strawberry plants, 45 minutes

How? Choose a sunny or partially shaded spot in well-cultivated soil, preferably to which garden compost or manure has been added. Make a hole for each plant about 30 cm (12 in) apart and place the plant into it, spreading out the spider-like roots so that they aren't cramped. Firm in and water well.

Make sure you: Try to position the 'crown' of the plant – the pointy bit in the centre from where new leaves grow – so it sits on the surface of the soil. If you bury the crown, it has a tendency to rot. If you plant it too high, it might dry out.

What next? Keep moist as the plants establish. When little fruits start to form feed plants in containers every fortnight with a liquid seaweed feed. At the end of the summer when the leaves turn yellow, cut them back to about 10 cm (4 in) above the crown to keep them tidy and disease free over winter (except with 'ever-bearing' varieties, which you can just leave as they are). You'll want to replace ground-grown plants every three years and container-grown plants every two, to keep getting a decent crop. This is no real hassle, since you can easily get new plants by rooting the runners.

Where have I gone wrong? Slugs and snails (*see page 36*) are your number one enemies when it comes to strawberries. I swear they're telepathic. Again and again, I've had my eye on a perfect-looking fruit and thought I'll give that just one more day so it's really sweet. Invariably, the next day will dawn and I'll discover a snail or slug hole right in the middle. Be vigilant.

Barefoot Breakfast Smoothie

You wake up on a summer's weekday morning with half an hour to get yourself together and out of the house. Float outside, barely dressed, pick a handful of perfectly ripe strawberries and, within minutes, you are drinking an exquisitely refreshing, vitamin-packed smoothie that'll set you up for the day and still give you enough time to catch your train. This recipe is so easy you can prepare it in five minutes. You can replace the strawberries with raspberries, blueberries, blackberries or any mix of the above. You can't really go wrong - pretty much any combination tastes delicious.

Serves 1
4 large ice cubes
6 or more ripe strawberries
2 heaped tbsp Greek yogurt
1 tbsp runny honey
mint sprig, optional

Wrap the ice cubes in a clean tea towel and bash them with a rolling pin until they have become a fine snow (this is much less hard work than it sounds). Roughly chop the strawberries and put them in a bowl with the yogurt, crushed ice and honey, then whizz it all up for a few seconds with a blender (a hand-held one is fine) until it's smooth. Taste and add more honey if it's not sweet enough.

If you're feeling decorative, add a halved strawberry on top. If you're really pushing the boat out for guests, you could even throw on a sprig of mint.

SUMMER ESSENTIALS

How to water

I knew I had finally reached gardening obsessed the other day while watching a police drama on TV. The suspect was watering flowers in his garden by sprinkling their petals with a watering can in the heat of the afternoon. 'No,' I all but yelled at the screen, 'you're torturing them!' I can't remember whodunit in the end, but I know who was guilty of crimes against flowers.

Follow these watering tips and your plants will thank you for it:

Water the compost around the plants, not the plants themselves. It's the roots that need water, not the leaves.

Water in the morning or evening on hot days. If you water when the sun is shining, you can scorch the leaves and flowers. You'll also lose a lot through evaporation.

Soak the roots rather than just give them a vague sprinkle. A few seconds with your thumb over the hose will barely wet the surface.

Wigwams, obelisks and other pretty things to climb up

Runner beans, sweet peas, squashes, French (green) beans, cucumbers, courgettes (zucchinis) and peas can be a wonderful sight climbing up a wigwam or clambering over a pergola or arch. Pop them in garden soil or the centre of pots on a balcony and you've got instant height. They're also a great way to grow a lot of crops in a small space.

Ready-made obelisks or wigwams can be bought in garden centres and aren't expensive. All you do is push them into the ground and you're away. Or you can make them yourself by pushing five bamboo canes into the ground in a rough circle and tying them together at the top. If you want a modern, urban look go for metal obelisks or maypole climbing frames, on which plants climb up strings pegged into the ground around a black steel pole. For a looser, more cottage-garden style, choose willow or hazel

obelisks. I leave mine in the ground all winter, since they look great, even when they're bare. Arches are another quick and easy way to add height. You can buy fairly cheap willow and steel ones ready-made. Just push into the ground over a pathway, grow squashes, beans and roses over them and you've got an instant cottagey feature.

Whatever sort of structure you go for, do make sure you push it into the ground securely before you plant anything and choose a sheltered spot. It's easy to underestimate the weight of a wigwam full of runner beans, especially when there's a wind blowing. I lost all my beans last summer when the wigwam was toppled, ripping the poor things out at the roots. The scars still linger.

To help plants climb up fences or walls it's a good idea to fix some trellis. It saves no end of fiddly tying in of wires and strings, since climbers will clamber up it with the ease of a Sherpa.

Do I have to go to the beach now?

I keep banging on about 'liquid seaweed' in this book. Before you think you need to head to the coast and fill a carrier bag with bladderwrack, let me explain that seaweed feed is available in bottles at any garden centre. All you have to do is put a capful in a watering can of water and pour it onto the compost around any fruit or vegetable plant. How often? It depends, but usually once every week or fortnight (don't worry if you're not exact, plants don't have watches).

I used to mentally skim over the bits in gardening books that talked about feeding plants. It all sounded so technical, surely involving smelly powders and weird measuring equipment. But then I bought some tomato food from a shop (the bottle had a big picture of tomatoes on it, it wasn't hard) and realized this feeding business is just a question of pouring a capful of dark brown stuff into a watering can and pouring it on.

If you don't feed your plants nothing terrible will happen. They won't die. But they won't produce so

many tomatoes, chillis, courgettes (zucchinis) or strawberries, the ones they do produce won't be as big, healthy and tasty, and the plant won't crop for as long. Just get plant food that says it's for fruit or flowers; any that calls itself tomato food will do the job. I like liquid seaweed feeds because they're organic and they work. Also, I'm squeamish. There are all manner of ghoulish-sounding fertilizers out there. The Victorians used rotten fish mashed up with a spade. Old timers on allotments swear by chicken poo or blood, fish and bone. I think, on balance, you're getting off lightly with a very slight whiff of the seaside.

Don't cry over split tomatoes

Early in the season, my tomato fruits usually get eaten before they make it into the kitchen. But if their skins are split, don't throw them away. Roast them in the oven with garlic and olive oil – the perfect sweet, tangy accompaniment for lamb or sausages. Mix them up with feta cheese, olive oil, olives and thyme for a delicious Greek-style dish crying out to be mopped up with fresh French bread. Or simmer them with onions, garlic and oregano for a delicious simple pasta sauce.

WHEN LOOKS MATTER

Feel free to bung your plants in willy-nilly. Any plant that's healthy is going to look fairly appealing, wherever you put it. But sometimes it's fun to try and get a bit artistic. The only danger is that, once you start, you become obsessed and refuse to pick that red lettuce because it'll ruin the symmetry of your red-and-green-salad chequerboard bed. If this happens, I'm afraid I can't help you, you're a lost cause.

The height of perfection

Vary the heights when you're planting up a bed. Some plants are so big they act as centrepieces all on their own, such as globe artichokes and feathery bronze fennel, which can rear up to almost 2 m (6 ft). Or grow runner beans, sweet peas or trailing nasturtiums, cucumbers or squashes up wigwams. Ready-made arches and pergolas are worth thinking about too *(see Wigwams, obelisks and other pretty things to climb up, page 74).*

 ## Cheat's tip: picking tomatoes

Of course, you can pick tomatoes any way you like, but the quickest and easiest way to harvest them without damaging them is to push down on the crooked 'knuckle' of stem holding each tomato to the vine. This way you pick them complete with the calyx (green star bit on the top of the tomato) and avoid splitting the skin so they'll keep longer. It also makes a nice, clean little snap noise that I find strangely satisfying. But maybe that's just me.

Cheat's tip: plugging the gap

So you've spent the spring sowing lovely seeds and now have a patio or garden full of growing plants, right? ... Right? Sometimes life doesn't work out as we hope. Maybe you've been busy at work. Maybe you were on holiday. Or you just didn't get round to it. Just because you haven't been nurturing seedlings on your windowsill for the past month or so doesn't mean you can't have a garden full of burgeoning salad, herbs, vegetables and fruit this summer. Garden centres and online plant companies (see *Little Green Book, page 140*) have all manner of little plants available, ready-grown. They're a fantastically easy way to get your edible garden up and running over a weekend. They may not allow you quite the number of varieties that you get when growing your own from seed, but the choice is improving every day. Cheating? Who's ever going to know?

Do my carrots go with my shoes?

Just like flowers, the colours and textures of vegetables and fruit plants vary wildly and you can create some really dramatic combinations. Try bright and unusually coloured varieties – purple French (green) beans, 'Tromboncino' squashes, black tomatoes, yellow mangetout (snow peas) or purple artichokes. Contrast feathery patches of carrots with glossy, large-leaved chard. Make the most of striking structural plants, such as the delicate plume of feathery fennel, whether the green or bronze sort, and contrast with big, bold brassicas or lush-leaved aubergines (eggplants). Salad leaves look particularly varied – from purple to green, frilly to pointed. Plant them in wavy lines, crosses, triangles, squares, chequerboards... Who knew you could express yourself so much with lettuce?

Wall huggers

Artfully clothe your fences or walls not only with blackberries, flowering climbers or trained fruit trees, such as espalier apples or fan-trained plums, cherries and peaches, but also with tomatoes, growing up strings tied to the top of the fence. Runner and climbing beans and squashes will also scramble up trellis, as will sweet peas, cucumbers and climbing courgettes (zucchinis).

Mix n match

If things start looking boring, add a flower, that's my motto. My garden is roughly two-thirds fruit and vegetables, one-third flowers, and it's a ratio that seems to work. In the height of summer when the cosmea, alliums and nicotiana are waving high and the nasturtiums a sea of orange, you might not think there were any edible crops in there at all.

Edging

An edging of curly parsley, thyme, chives, spiky rocket (arugula), oriental greens or strawberries can look rather stylish. Choose plants that are low-growing (so you can see over them to the bed behind) and non-spreading so they keep their neat pattern.

Home-grown Pesto Sauce

Use your own freshly picked basil leaves and even your own garlic in this great, quick lunch full of the flavours of summer.

Serves 2
1 handful of pine nuts
6 tbsp roughly chopped, freshly picked basil leaves
½ garlic clove
1 handful of freshly grated Parmesan cheese
olive oil
sea salt and ground black pepper

Lightly toast the pine nuts in a dry frying pan for 2–3 minutes. Blend them in a processor with the basil, garlic and Parmesan. Slowly blend in olive oil in stages until it's a thick, gloopy consistency. Season to taste. Stir the sauce into cooked and drained hot pasta and sprinkle with more Parmesan if you like.

Weekend Project: It's all Greek to Me

Who doesn't love a Greek salad on a summer's day? Plant up these pots and recreate its classic mixture of juicy tomatoes, crunchy cucumber, lettuce and oregano on your patio. All you'll need are the feta cheese and black Kalamata olives.

You will need
2 large pots with drainage holes,
at least 45 cm (18 in) diameter
multipurpose compost
1 small obelisk
garden twine
2 cucumber plants – an outdoor
variety such as 'Burpless Tasty Green'
7 or more lettuce seedlings – a mini cos
type such as 'Little Gem' or 'Pinokkio'
1 packet of salad or spring onion (scallion)
seeds such as 'White Lisbon'
2 bush tomato plants such as
'Red Alert' or 'Tumbling Tom'
1 Greek oregano plant
1 hour

Add a layer of crocks to the bottom of both pots and almost fill them with compost. In one pot, push the obelisk into the middle, then plant the cucumber plants either side of it, loosely tying in the stems to the frame. Plant your lettuce seedlings around the edge of the pot about 15 cm (6 in) apart in any remaining space. Then sprinkle a pinch of spring onion (scallion) seeds into the gaps between the lettuces and barely cover with compost. In the other pot, plant the tomato plants and oregano. Firm all the plants in and water well.

Water regularly and feed every two weeks with liquid seaweed. When the onion seedlings are big enough to handle, thin them to about 3 cm (1 in) apart, eating the thinnings. When the cucumber plants have five or six leaves, pinch out the growing tip to encourage sideshoots to grow and tie these in to the obelisk. When fruits appear on the cucumber and tomatoes, feed fortnightly with liquid seaweed.

Planting out tomatoes

When all risk of frost has passed – early summer is a safe bet – it's time to plant out your tomato seedlings. Once little fruits start to appear, feed the plants every fortnight with tomato food or liquid seaweed.

In garden soil

Choose a sunny, sheltered spot in which the soil is well-cultivated and has been enriched with garden compost or manure. The 'sunny spot' bit is important – to ripen sweetly, these southern hemisphere fruits really do need some heat.

By far the simplest way to support upright tomatoes is to plant them near a wall or fence and tie a length of string from the top of it. Twirl it around the stem of the plant a couple of times. Then, as it grows, twirl it round again every week or so – it's surprising how strong a support this is even for a mature plant heavy with fruit.

Upright tomato plants can also look pretty growing up obelisks in the centre of a bed. If you want to make it really look the business, cover the feet of the tomatoes and any bare soil with one or two nasturtium plants for a froth of orange and yellow flowers or a courgette (zucchini) plant that will soon give a deep green sea of leaves.

In containers

Plant one bush tomato plant or three upright ones in a pot at least 30 cm (12 in) in diameter, tied in to a wigwam of bamboo canes. Three upright tomatoes are happy in a growing bag tied into bamboo canes or supported by a string hanging down from the fence. Trailing forms of bush tomatoes such as 'Tumbling Tom' or 'Red Alert' will cascade beautifully over the side of a hanging basket or window box. Plant one plant in each hanging basket in multipurpose compost. **What next?** Upright tomato plants grow straight upwards with leaves and fruit coming directly off the main stem. However, they also tend to produce shoots in the joints between some of the leaves and the stem. If left to develop, these will sprawl all over the place and divert away energy that you need to be focused on the developing fruits and growing tip of the main stem. So you 'pinch them out' – simply breaking them off between thumb and forefinger. Once you've got the hang of it, it's surprisingly satisfying and weirdly addictive…

Water your tomatoes often – perhaps every day at the height of summer. Those in growing bags and pots are particularly vulnerable to drying out. Once an entire truss of tomatoes has been harvested, remove the leaves below this truss. This discourages disease and lets the sun in. Once each plant has formed five trusses of tomatoes, pinch off the top of your plants one leaf above the top flower truss. This gives these trusses a chance to ripen before autumn sets in.

Where have I gone wrong? Tomatoes are relatively trouble free, but they can occasionally suffer from whitefly and aphid damage and then, later in the season, blossom end rot and blight. *See Edible Garden Enemies, page 134.*

Runner beans

DIFFICULTY RATING

Look, I know what you're thinking. These are what granddads grow. Well, maybe they do. Runner beans are the archetypal crop of the traditional allotment, often seen growing next to an old man drinking nettle wine and wearing sandals over his socks. But let me try to rehabilitate this most misunderstood of vegetables. Yes, they're an old-fashioned favourite, and yes, you may have been given them as a child and thought they tasted like leather bookmarks because they'd been boiled for half an hour. But slice them into succulent ribbons using one of those handy bean slicers, steam or boil them for a few minutes and top with butter, salt and pepper, and I don't think there's anything I look forward to so much in my garden. Apart from tomatoes of course, but then tomatoes are in a league of their own. Runner beans are perhaps the prettiest crop you can grow. With their bright scarlet flowers, heart-shaped leaves, dangling kipper-tie-like beans and ability to clamber in a picturesque fashion up wigwams and obelisks, they're a must-have for anyone who wants looks as well as lunch. A single wigwam will keep you in beans from midsummer right up to the first frosts. They're also at home in slight shade, so great for those who don't have entirely sunny gardens.

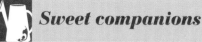

Sweet companions

I often plant sweet peas (*see page 61*) at the base of the same wigwam since they combine beautifully with the beans and flower much earlier so there's something lovely to look at from early summer.

I'm a fan of 'Painted Lady' with its delicate red and white flowers, and 'Scarlet Emperor', which has bright red flowers and very tasty and prolific pods. Other good varieties are 'Enorma' and 'Red Rum'. For planting in containers, 'Hestia' is particularly good since it grows only to about 50 cm (20 in).

Sowing runner beans

When? Early summer

In pots

YOU WILL NEED

A medium to large, fairly deep container with drainage holes, multipurpose compost, a small obelisk or five bamboo canes, garden twine, runner bean seeds, 30 minutes

How? Add a layer of crocks to the bottom of the container and then fill it almost to the top with compost. If you are sowing a climbing variety, either push your

Weekend Project: Beanfest in a Box

Crunchy salad, beans and glorious colour all in the same box. You can use green dwarf French (green) beans, but there's something deliciously striking about the purple ones. The dashing orange of the marigolds contrasts beautifully with the purple beans and bright green salad leaves. If you don't want to use a window box, all these plants will fit in a 45 cm (18 in) diameter pot.

You will need
1 large window box with drainage holes, at least 60 cm (2 ft) long and 20 cm (8 in) deep multipurpose compost
3 dwarf French (green) bean plants, preferably purple-podded such as 'Purple Teepee'
6 'Little Gem' lettuce seedlings
3 golden marigold plants such as calendula officinalis (though any would be fine)
1 hour

Add a layer of crocks to the bottom of the box and then fill it almost to the top with compost. Plant the bean plants along the back and the marigolds in front of them, then fill the remaining space with the lettuce seedlings. Either wait for the lettuces to mature before cutting them or pick off leaves as and when you want them. Strew a few marigold petals on top of your salad for the height of home-grown elegance. Water well and place on a sunny windowsill. Deadhead the marigolds regularly to keep a supply of flowers.

ready-made obelisk into the compost or push in the bamboo canes in a rough circle and tie them together at the top. Push the seeds into the compost to a depth of about 5 cm (2 in), one seed either side of each cane or upright support. If you've bought ready-grown plants, space them about 10 cm (4 in) apart. Dwarf varieties need no supports, simply sow them about 10 cm (4 in) apart (a 30 cm/12 in diameter pot would take five plants). Water. Place in a sunny or partially shaded spot.

In garden soil

YOU WILL NEED

An obelisk or five bamboo canes, garden twine, runner bean seeds, 30 minutes

How? Choose a sunny or partially shaded spot with well-cultivated soil that has preferably had manure or compost added the previous year. Somewhere out of the wind is ideal. Push your obelisk or bamboo canes into the soil as deep as you can, tying the canes together at the top, to prevent the wind blowing them over. For sowing instructions, see above.

What next? Keep a close eye out for slugs and snails at the early stages – they love baby runner bean plants and can munch through a whole stem in one night. I can't count the number of times I've pondered over the reason for a limp-looking stem only to realize that it's been chopped cleanly through halfway down. Throughout the summer keep the beans well watered – particularly if growing in a container – and feed with liquid seaweed every three weeks or so. Once the plants reach the top of the wigwam, pinch out the tops.

Where have I gone wrong? Apart from keeping an eye on slugs and snails (*see page 36*), the only thing that tends to be a problem for runner beans is poor pollination. This is when you get loads of flowers but not many beans. This could be caused by not watering enough or cold and windy weather, which puts bees off their pollinating stride. When the weather improves, the number of beans usually does too.

French (green) beans

This is the bean of the classic Nicoise salad, otherwise known as 'that bean in the cellophane packs flown in from thousands of miles away'. We've all thrown these into our trolleys after a hard day and felt a little bit guilty about our eco footprint. Grow your own and you'll gain significant air mile smug points. Chop the ends off, line them up like little soldiers and wrap them in clingfilm if it makes you happier.

French (green) beans make lovely-looking plants, particularly striking in large pots or window boxes, where a mix of the purple, yellow and green varieties together is rather gorgeous. Choose a nice, sheltered spot for these tender creatures and only sow when summer has got into its stride. Climbing forms wind their way up canes, covered in little pink flowers, while the dwarf sorts form a dense jungly mat of leaves.

Grow the climbing varieties, such as 'Blue Lake' and 'Cobra', yellow 'Neckargold' and purple 'Blauhilde' up canes like runner beans. Or why not try 'Borlotti Lingua di Fuoco', an Italian climbing bean with spectacular bright red and green-flecked

pods? If you don't have the space, dwarf varieties such as 'Safari', 'Tendergreen', 'Purple Teepee' and vivid yellow 'Rocquencourt' are all happy in pots where their heart-shaped leaves and clusters of dangling beans are bountiful summer itself.

Keep picking and they'll keep producing, but for a constant supply sow a handful of seeds every fortnight.

Sowing French (green) beans

When? Early to late summer

In pots

YOU WILL NEED

A medium to large container with drainage holes, multipurpose compost, french (green) bean seeds, an obelisk or 5 bamboo canes, garden twine (if a climbing variety), 20 minutes

How? Sow as for runner beans (*see page 81*), though you can sow them slightly closer together. A 30 cm (12 in) diameter pot could take 6–8 plants.

In garden soil

YOU WILL NEED

French (green) bean seeds, an obelisk or five bamboo canes, garden twine (if a climbing variety), 20 minutes

How? Sow as for runner beans (*see page 81*), though French (green) beans need a sunnier spot.
What next? As climbing varieties start to grow, twirl them round the canes to help them to cling on. Keep a close eye out for slugs and snails and keep well watered, especially those in containers. Once the little beans start to form, feed fortnightly with liquid seaweed.
Where have I gone wrong? Watch out for slugs and snails *(see page 36)* and blackfly *(see Edible Garden Enemies, page 134).*

Planting out aubergines (eggplants), sweet peppers and chillis

If you sowed these inside in mid-spring or have bought plants from a garden centre, early summer is the time to plant them out. They do best in containers, but what sort is up to you. If you choose a window box, make it a large, deep one since they need a decent root run. If you choose a pot, make it no less than 25 cm (10 in) in diameter for each plant. If a growing bag, cut three holes in the top and plant two aubergines (eggplants) or three chilli or sweet pepper plants. If you don't plant a compact variety, you may need to provide bamboo canes to support plants as they grow.

Plant in multipurpose compost, water well and place in the hottest, most sheltered spot in your garden. When the first little fruits start to form, feed the plants fortnightly with liquid seaweed.

For harvesting sweet peppers and chillis, *see left and Bring in the heat lovers, page 107.*

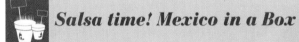

Salsa time! Mexico in a Box

Here's one for fajita fans. Grow this collection of sweet, succulent tomatoes and crunchy lettuce, onions, fiery chillis and coriander (cilantro) for fresh, delicious fillings for Mexican classics such as tacos and tortillas. If you don't want to use a window box, divide the plants between a couple of large (at least 45 cm/18 in diameter pots) instead.

You will need
1 large window box with drainage holes, at least 80 cm (2½ ft) long and as deep as possible
multipurpose compost
2 bush tomato plants such as 'Red Alert' or 'Tumbling Tom'
1 chilli plant – any dwarf or container variety such as 'Etna'
1 coriander (cilantro) plant
5–6 lettuce seedlings – a small, crunchy variety such as 'Little Gem' is ideal
salad onion (scallion) seed such as 'White Lisbon'
40 minutes

Add a layer of crocks to the bottom of the box and two-thirds fill with compost. Making small holes in the compost, plant the tomatoes and chilli at the back, with the tomatoes in the corners and chilli in the middle. Fill with compost so the plants are at the same level as they were in their pots. Plant the coriander (cilantro) in one of the front corners and then the lettuce seedlings along the front of the box about 15 cm (6 in) apart. Finally, sprinkle a pinch of salad onion (scallion) seeds in each of the gaps between the lettuces. Cover thinly with compost. Water well and place on a sunny windowsill.

When the salad onion (scallion) seedlings are big enough to handle, thin so they are about 3 cm (1 in) apart (eat the thinnings in salad, they're delicious). Keep the box well watered and feed it every couple of weeks with liquid seaweed. Resow the salad onions and replant the lettuce and coriander (cilantro) if needed to keep a constant supply throughout the summer. Leave the tomato plants to trail over the sides.

Blueberries

I'm sure it was the blueberry that saved me. It was a particularly bleak summer cold. My head was like achy cotton wool, my eyes sore, my nose streaming, and I couldn't face leaving the house to buy orange juice let alone Paracetamol. Yet instinct drew me to the garden where I threw handfuls of blueberries into my mouth like a Californian vitamin junkie at breakfast. I swear I felt better by the end of the day (though six hours in front of the television may also have helped).

Blueberries have indeed been declared a superfood, packed with age-defying antioxidants, vitamin C, flavanoids and even something that prevents the formation of wrinkles. I suspect they may be able to speak foreign languages. Even if they weren't such a wonder berry, though, I'd have a couple of bushes in the garden. They're so low maintenance you can ignore them all year and still get handsome foliage, delicate cream or pink flowers and a crop of beautiful, sweet berries in return. They don't even take up much space.

I have three blueberries in my little garden and they're up there with my favourite plants in the garden. They need no pruning apart from the removal of dead twigs, can be left outside all winter and are largely untroubled by pests. 'Bluecrop', 'Spartan' and 'Earliblue' are all reliable, but the semi-evergreen ones, such as 'Sunshine Blue' and 'Toro' are the prettiest because their leaves turn a beautiful auburn in the autumn and brighten up the garden all winter.

Planting blueberries

Grow blueberries in a pot because they will only grow in ericaceous compost – available from all garden centres. Plant your blueberry bush in a container at least 30 cm (12 in) in diameter in ericaceous compost and put it in a sunny position. Being acid-loving plants, blueberries should, strictly speaking, be watered with rainwater, not tap. But don't worry too much about this. I've always watered mine from the garden hose and they've been laden with berries. From early summer, when the flowers start to set fruit, give the bush a fortnightly feed with a tomato feed or liquid seaweed.

Globe artichokes

Architectural, stately and downright huge, these plants look majestic at the back or centre of a bed, rearing up above everything else. Somehow they make your garden look rather grand, however tiny it is. Just a couple is enough for most town gardens since a mature plant can take up 1 m (3 ft) of your precious space and grow up to 2 m (6? ft) high (not one for containers, then). Expect up to 12 artichokes from each mature plant. Their spiny artichokes – actually flower buds that have yet to open – wave above long, beautiful, silvery-green serrated leaves. Buy ready-grown plants. They should last for a good few years.

'Green Globe' is a good variety to go for, though real show-offs might prefer the purple-headed 'Violetto di Chioggia'. Cut the heads while still small to eat whole or leave them to mature, then boil and eat them dipped in melted butter or mayonnaise. If you can bear to leave any on the plant, they'll reward you with beautiful, purple, thistle-like flowers.

Planting globe artichokes

When? Early summer to midsummer

Where? Outside in garden soil, which has had plenty of garden compost or well-rotted manure added, in a sunny, sheltered spot. Globe artichokes hate being waterlogged so if you have a heavy clay soil, also add some grit to improve the drainage.

YOU WILL NEED

A globe artichoke plant, 20 minutes

How? Dig a hole big enough for your artichoke plant, allowing a couple of feet around it for the plant to grow. Place the plant in the hole and then firm in, cover with soil and water well.

What next? It feels a shame, I know, but to get a really strong plant, you should cut off all buds the plant produces in its first summer. From then on, harvest the buds when they reach a size you like eating. In the spring, mulch your plants with garden compost.

Where have I gone wrong? When your plants are young, watch out for slugs and snails (*see page 36*). Feeble growth and rotting leaves in young plants are a sign of bad drainage – dig in some grit.

Weekend Project: Thai Tor Two

Dig out your Thai fishing trousers and recreate that pad thai you had on the Khao San Road. Here's all you need to bring the flavours of Bangkok to soups, stir-fries or curries. Line up coriander (cilantro), mulberry-edged Thai basil, a plume of fragrant lemon grass and a glossy chilli plant for that important blast of heat. Finish it all off with a pot of crunchy pak choi. Rather than cram all these plants in a window box, they'll benefit from being in separate pots so could just as easily be arranged on a patio or balcony.

You will need
4 pots with drainage holes, at least 20 cm (8 in) in diameter
1 pot with drainage holes, at least 30 cm (18 in) in diameter multipurpose compost
4 pak choi plants
1 chilli pepper plant suitable for container growing, such as 'Etna'. If you were being strictly Thai, you would grow Thai bird's eye chilli, but any compact variety will do
1 pot of Thai basil (Ocimum basilicum 'Horapha Nanum')
1 lemon grass plant
1 pot of coriander (cilantro)
30 minutes

Add a layer of crocks to the bottom of the pots and then fill them almost to the top with compost. Transplant the pak choi plants into the larger pot, firm in well and water. Then transplant the chilli, basil, lemon grass and coriander (cilantro) into the remaining pots. Place them on a sunny windowsill or patio and water well.
Pinch out the growing tips (and eat them) of the basil from early summer onwards to encourage it to bush up. Resow or replant the coriander (cilantro) when needed – it's a short-lived plant and doesn't resprout when the leaves are cut. Feed the chilli weekly with a high-potash feed

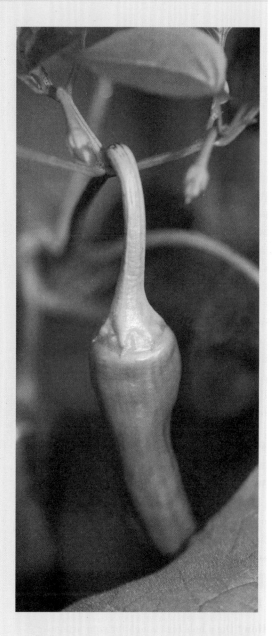

such as liquid seaweed when it starts to set fruit. In autumn, bring it and the lemon grass inside to a sunny windowsill so that the peppers can fully ripen and the lemon grass can survive the winter.

SUMMER JOBS

Give a fig about pruning

That high-maintenance specimen the fig tree needs a little attention in early summer. The new shoots should be growing well by now but you don't want the tree to put all its energy into growing long shoots, you want it to plump up those tiny, new fig fruit buds. So pinch out each new shoot so that only five leaves remain. You should be able to do this with your thumb and forefinger.

A plum job

Plums are such pleasers – they produce far too many plums and then exhaust themselves so much they don't produce anything the following year. Do them a favour by thinning the fruit in midsummer so you are left with one plum every 5 cm (2 in). It's agony to throw away healthy fruit, I know, but it's better than having no plums next year.

Show raspberries who's boss

If you have autumn-fruiting raspberry canes they'll be getting tall and a bit sprawling by now. Push in some bamboo canes and tie the raspberry canes to them to keep the bush tidy. Also keep an eye out for errant new canes – raspberries love to colonize new areas – and dig up any that have strayed too far from the original bush with a hand trowel and compost them.

Sow Florence Fennel

This aniseedy, succulent white bulb with feathery leaves is gorgeous sliced paper-thin and eaten raw in salads, or braised, but you really need to wait until midsummer to sow it because it has a nasty habit of bolting (running to seed) if temperatures drop. Choose Romanesco and sow direct into garden soil or pots 1cm deep, then thin seedlings to 20cm (8in) apart. Harvest in early autumn.

Weekend Project: Ratatouille Riot

Bring the flavours of Provence to your patio with this rambunctious collection of big, hearty Mediterranean heat lovers. Give these tomatoes, courgettes (zucchinis), aubergines (eggplants), peppers and oregano a sun-drenched spot and you could be recreating the classic French stew by late summer.

You will need
2 large containers with drainage holes –
old wooden wine crates (see page 10)
are ideal, or divide your plants between
2 large pots at least 45 cm (18 in) in
diameter or 2 large window boxes at least 80
cm (2½ ft) long
multipurpose compost
1 tomato plant – a bush, tumbling variety such
as 'Tumbling Tom'

1 aubergine (eggplant) plant – a dwarf baby
variety such as 'Ophelia' or 'Orlando'
1 sweet pepper plant – a dwarf variety
such as 'Redskin'
1 courgette (zucchini) plant – a compact
variety such as 'Tuscany' or 'Defender'
1 thyme plant
40 minutes

Add a layer of crocks to the bottom of your containers and half fill them with compost. Arrange the plants on the compost as you want them, remembering to allow room for the tomato and courgette (zucchini) to trail, then fill the containers almost to the top, firming the plants in well. Water well. Place in a sunny position and feed every fortnight with tomato feed or liquid seaweed.

Weekend Project: The Essential Salad Box

This classic salad collection is super easy to grow and always rises to the occasion. Two compact bush tomato plants, fragrant basil and a row of lush oak-leaf lettuce will keep you in salad all summer. All you need is the dressing.

You will need
1 large window box with drainage holes
multipurpose compost
2 bush tomato plants such as 'Red Alert' or 'Tumbling Tom'
1 'Sweet Genovese' basil plant
1 packet of 'Green Oak Leaf' lettuce seed (or any lettuce)
40 minutes

Add a layer of crocks to the bottom of the window box and then fill it almost to the top with compost. Making holes in the compost, plant the tomato plants at either end of the box and the basil in the middle, then sprinkle the lettuce seed thinly over any remaining space. Barely cover with a sprinkle of compost. Water well.

As the plants grow, keep the compost moist. Harvest the lettuce as baby leaves by cutting just above the smallest new leaf with scissors when the plants are about 10 cm (4 in) high. Resow the lettuce when the plants stop growing strongly. Feed the tomato every fortnight with a tomato feed or liquid seaweed once fruits have started to form.

Harvesting garlic

Depending on the variety, any garlic that you planted in autumn (*see page 110*) will be ready to harvest from late spring (for example, 'Early Wight') to midsummer (for example, 'Albigensian Wight'). Keep an eye on the leaves and when they start to turn yellow have an experimental root around to see how big the bulbs have become. If they're still small, keep them well watered to help swell and have another look in a week or so.

If you're happy with the size of the bulbs, carefully dig up the bulb with a trowel, leaves and all. If it is a hardneck or short-storing variety, such as 'Early Wight' or 'Purple Wight', you'll want to use your garlic fresh, so simply use it as you wish (it makes a glorious chicken and very garlicky soup). For longer-storing varieties, hang the bulbs up by the leaves somewhere warm and dry. After about three weeks, when the leaves rustle and the skin of the bulbs has turned papery, they are ready to store. This is when you locate your inner medieval French peasant and plait the leaves together. If, like me, that is beyond your weaving skills, just loosely tie the leaves together and hang your bunch of garlic up in the kitchen within reach of a chopping board. It should keep for months, during which time friends will gaze admiringly at your home-grown harvest and say 'Wow, did you grow all that?' to which the correct response is to nod modestly.

Planting out courgettes (zucchinis)

Once all risk of frost has passed, it's safe to pop your courgette (zucchini) plants out into their final growing positions. Choose a sunny spot with well-cultivated soil that has had manure or garden compost added. Plant climbing varieties at the base of obelisks or a trellised fence so you can tie them in as they grow. Give bush varieties a good 50 cm (20 in) of space around them in garden borders so they can sprawl happily. Or plant compact varieties in large pots (one plant to a pot at least 45cm/18 in in diameter) or growing bags (two per bag).

What next? Keep well watered and, once the first flowers appear, feed fortnightly with liquid seaweed. Harvest the courgettes (zucchinis) when they're about 10 cm (4 in) long. Leave them too long and you'll be faced with a marrow. And, believe me, nobody wants that. As I discovered to my cost one summer, there's only so many ways you can fill a 'marrow boat'.

Where have I gone wrong? Courgettes (zucchinis) are easy to grow, but problems could include slugs and snails *(see page 36)* and powdery mildew *(see Edible Garden Enemies, page 134)*. Poor pollination, in which fruits start to grow but then rot from the ends, can also cause consternation if there is a cold early summer when few pollinating insects are about. The good news is that the problem will improve when the weather does, but if you want to take a more proactive approach, try pollinating the flowers by hand *(see Cheat's tip: Do I hear the patter of tiny pumpkins? below)*.

Planting out cucumbers

Cucumbers are not quite as rampaging as courgettes (zucchinis), but they're still quite greedy, so, if you're planting them in garden soil, choose a spot that has

had manure or garden compost added to it. They need a sunny, sheltered position to feel happy. Plant two at the base of an obelisk and, when they have five or six leaves, pinch out the tips of the plants to encourage sideshoots to grow. Tie these in to the obelisk. If growing in a pot, make sure it's at least 30 cm (12 in) in diameter and grow up an obelisk, or plant two in a growing bag and tie in to bamboo canes. You could also try one plant in a hanging basket or deep window box and let the plant trail down rather than climb up.

What next? When the fruits appear, feed fortnightly with liquid seaweed. Pick the cucumbers when they're no more than 12 cm (5 in) long and peel them before eating.

Where have I gone wrong? Cucumbers suffer from the same ills as courgettes (zucchinis). *See Courgettes (Zucchinis): where have I gone wrong? see left.*

Planting out squashes and pumpkins

Just one or two squash vines are enough for most small gardens or patios. Everything about these plants is big, especially their appetites. Choose a sunny, sheltered spot where the soil has been well

---

🪣 *Cheat's tip: do I hear the patter of tiny pumpkins?*

In an ideal world, every baby courgette (zucchini), squash or pumpkin would develop into a lovely big fruit. In a less than perfect summer, however, there might not be the number of bees around needed to pollinate the female flowers so they grow to a certain size, then rot and fall off. This is where you may need to lend a helping hand. We're talking hand pollination, people. I've updated the traditional tool for this job – a rabbit's tail – to a cotton wool ball since that's what I'm more likely to have in my bathroom cabinet. You could also use a soft brush like a make-up brush, but you'll get pollen in your

foundation. Gently dab the cotton wool ball inside a male flower (one with a thin stem behind it), trying to get some pollen on the cotton wool. Then dab it inside a female flower (with the beginnings of a fruit swelling behind the bloom).

cultivated and manure or garden compost added, and feed every couple of weeks when fruits appear with liquid seaweed.

Plant near a wall or fence and encourage them to clamber up trellis by tying in the shoots as they grow. You could also plant one at the base of an obelisk or wigwam and tie it up and round it to make a pretty focal point in the centre of a bed or tub. Or just let them stretch out and sprawl in the sun. If you're planting in a container, choose a compact variety such as 'Baby Bear' and make it a big pot (at least 45 cm/ 18 in in diameter), or plant two in a growing bag. **What next?** When the plants have five or six leaves, pinch out the growing tips to encourage sideshoots to grow. For summer squashes such as 'Sunburst', pick when they're about the size of an apple. Leave winter squashes and pumpkins on the plant until autumn *(see Harvesting squashes and pumpkins, page 104)*.

Where have I gone wrong? Squashes and pumpkins suffer from the same ills as courgettes (zucchnis). *See Courgettes (zucchinis): where have I gone wrong?, page 91.*

Planting out sweetcorn

Hot, hot, hot, that's how these plants like it. So choose a prime position and plant them in a grid pattern. This is essential because otherwise, they won't be able to pollinate themselves properly (they rely on wind blowing the male tassels onto the female silks of neighbouring plants). Plant them about 45 cm (18 in) apart each way, watch out for slugs and snails *(see page 36)* and keep them moist as they establish. When they get fairly tall, earth up the stems a bit to stabilize them against the wind. For harvesting instructions, *see Harvesting sweetcorn, see page 97.*

Chard times

You may already have sown the spinach-like 'Bright Lights', Rainbow or Swiss chard in the spring, but if you want to guarantee a welcome splash of colour and lush greenery in the garden all the way through

Herb Butter

Your herbs should be going great guns by midsummer, but by autumn some of them, such as chives and tarragon, will be running out of steam. Preserve summer by making delicious herb butters that can be sliced direct from the freezer and added to the top of steaks and vegetables in winter.

Makes 6 portions
1 handful of any soft green herb,
such as parsley, tarragon or
chives, chopped
175 g (6 oz) soft butter
1 tbsp lemon lemon juice

Beat the butter in a bowl until creamed. Add the herbs and lemon juice. Then place the herby butter on to clingfilm and roll it into a sausage shape. Put it in the freezer. When you want to use it, simply cut slices of butter as required, rewrap the rest with clingfilm and return to the freezer.

autumn and winter, sow in mid- to late summer too. Sow seed direct into garden soil or large containers for the patio and keep moist in the summer heat until established.

Tied to your blackberry?

If you're growing a blackberry against a wall or fence, it will be sending out long, loopy shoots by summer. Loop them up and down like a rollercoaster on one side of the base, tying them into parallel wires.

Radicchio

DIFFICULTY RATING

Added to milder-flavoured salad leaves in autumn and winter, these crunchy, red, slightly bitter leaves are great – particularly good with blue cheese, poached pears and walnuts. They're even better grilled, when their bitterness turns to sweetness. In the garden, whether in pots or soil, they provide a welcome dash of colour over the winter months, and an even more welcome harvest in early spring. As far as varieties go, 'Rosso di Treviso' is hard to beat, with deep burgundy leaves and striking white ribs.

Sowing radicchio

When? Midsummer

In pots

YOU WILL NEED

 A medium to large container with drainage holes, multipurpose compost, radicchio seeds, 20 minutes

How? Add a layer of crocks to the bottom of the container and then fill it almost to the top with compost. Sprinkle your seeds about 5 cm (2 in) apart over the surface, then cover with a thin layer of compost. Water. Place in a sunny or partially shaded spot.

In garden soil

YOU WILL NEED

A pencil or stick, radicchio seeds, 10 minutes

How? Choose a sunny spot with well-cultivated soil. With your pencil or stick, scratch a shallow groove in the soil. Sprinkle the radicchio seed along it about 5 cm (2 in) apart, then cover with soil and water well. **What next?** Keep moist. When the seedlings are big enough to handle thin them to about 20 cm (8 in) apart if growing in the ground. If growing in pots, thin to about six plants per 30 cm (12 in) diameter pot.

Harvest from autumn when the frosts turn the leaves from green to a lovely rich burgundy colour. *See also Harvesting radicchio, page 114.*

Where have I gone wrong? Radicchio doesn't tend to attract too many pests, but it doesn't like to be crowded. If you find your leaves turning brown and slimy, chances are they're too close together. Remove any slimy leaves, and thin seedlings to give them more space.

Cheat's tip: a tight fit for peaches

A peach ripening against a warm wall is a wonderful thing. You return to it daily to see how the red blush spreads over the creamy skin and it softens to an aromatic ripeness. Unfortunately, someone else is also watching. The damn birds… And the damn squirrels… And the damn mice. If you don't want to discover a half-gnawed peach on one of your inspections, better take precautions, and what better than some poorly chosen hosiery? We've all done it. Bought heinous tights and hidden them at the back of the drawer, wondering how we could ever have thought animal print would be a good look. Now you can use them for the power of good. Cut off the feet and put them over each individual peach. If you have sartorially erred as far as a pop sock, of course, this job is even easier. The critters will stay away. Take note, though, they may still get through a fish net. *See also Peaches and apricots, page 119.*

Lemons

Growing lemon trees is a favourite pastime of mine. I say 'growing lemon trees' rather than 'growing lemons' because, in truth, the actual harvest I've had from my citrus charge over the years could be described as, well, slim. But I'm hooked on the things. I fuss around my ten-year-old tree like a midwife, feeding it with its special feed, misting its leaves and admiring its flowers and tiny green lemons with a look of wonder. I've been known to remove scale insects from its leaves with my hands and squash them between my fingers. And all because of that fantasy of sitting in my garden on a warm summer's day, the scent of citrus blossom on the air, sipping a glass of Gin and tonic with a slice of my own lemon jostling with the ice cubes – a scenario that has, if I'm honest, only happened the once. Yes, growing lemon trees in a less than Mediterranean climate is a challenge.

Traditionally, lemon trees have been grown in conservatories, or at least brought inside into one for the winter. But these days, varieties such as 'Eureka' boast of being able to stay outside all year round. Certainly, my Meyer lemon has always survived uncovered, but you'd probably

get a better crop if you gave your tree a fleece jacket *(see page 118)* over the coldest months.

Lemons are needy. There is special food available from good nurseries – one for summer, one for winter. How high maintenance is that? They'll need the warmest, most sheltered spot on your terrace and also need to be planted in very free-draining soil – a John Innes compost with lots of perlite or grit. They're fussy about watering, liking a good drenching now and then rather than little and often. Oh, and did I mention they prefer rainwater to tap? If they were a person they'd be a Victorian maiden, prone to fainting spells and constantly needing her corset loosened.

So why do I persist in growing lemon trees and, more to the point, why am I recommending you do? Because they're beautiful trees – they look exotic with their glossy evergreen leaves and heavenly scented flowers – because they're a bit different, and because, you never know, one day you might be able to reach out from your dining chair and nonchalantly pick a perfect lemon and slice it into the glasses of your impressed guests. After all, there's got to be some upsides to global warming.

Other than the above varieties, other recommended lemons include 'La Valette' and 'Quatre Saisons'.

Planting lemons

Bought lemon trees can usually stay in the pot they came in for a season. Repot the following spring into a slightly larger pot filled with John Innes compost with a good few trowelfuls of grit. Keep your tree in a sunny, sheltered spot on the terrace.

Where have I gone wrong? Watch for scale insect and red spider mite. *See Edible Garden Enemies, page 134.*

Pak choi for the cold months

This oriental green is a fusspot about light and prone to bolting if sown in summer before Midsummer Day. But once that's over, it's well worth sowing a patch of pak choi either outside or in containers. It'll be a welcome source of lush, crunchy leafiness in the autumn and right up to midwinter when there's not much else around. For sowing instructions, *see Sowing pak choi, page 43.*

Planting out kale

By midsummer it's time to plant out kale. Your borders are probably jostling with plants by now, but it's worth finding some room for these beautiful brassicas because they'll bring some welcome life come winter when the garden is looking bare. They grow into big plants so ideally need to be planted about 30 cm (12 in) apart, but slot them in among other crops wherever you can. After all, by late autumn many crops will be removed, leaving the kales in splendid isolation. They like well-cultivated soil that has preferably had manure or garden compost added.

If your plants are destined for container growing, choose a pot at least 30 cm (12 in) in diameter for each plant as they can grow very big. To prettify the base of the plant, why not sow some nasturtiums around the edges of the pot? Three or four plug plants will be enough *(see page 60)*.

When planting them, firm them in well. The classic test is to pull the plant by a leaf. If the leaf tears before the plant is uprooted, you've planted it firmly enough.

Where have I gone wrong? Keep an eye out for slugs and snails *(see page 36)*, which can hide up in the leaf joints when the plant gets bigger, and caterpillars *(see Edible Garden Enemies, page 134)*.

Harvesting sweetcorn

By late summer, your cobs should be bulging out from the sides of your sweetcorn plants. I say 'should' because this is not the most reliable of crops in a changeable climate. Now you have to pick it just at the right moment.

Freeze some herbs

It's a great idea to freeze your herbs in their prime in ice-cube trays so you can enjoy your own fresh herbs all winter. Simply cut some, wash them, chop them up and add them to your ice-cube tray, then fill with water and freeze. You can then either defrost the cube to use the herbs or, as I do, just chuck them frozen into casseroles or sauces and watch them melt, releasing their freshly cut flavour even in the depths of winter.

I always get a bit anxious about timing the ripeness of sweetcorn because traditional advice makes it all sound rather critical. When the silks – the hair-like fronds coming out of the cob – start turning dark brown, they say, pull back the husk of the cob and jab your fingernail into one of the kernels. If the liquid is watery, it's still unripe. If it's doughy, it's overripe. If it's milky, it's just perfect. You'd think you were landing an airliner on the River Hudson, not picking a vegetable. Is it safe to pop to the shops, I wonder, or will I come back and find, God forbid, I've gone straight from watery to doughy and missed milky altogether? But maybe you're not such a natural worrier. Good luck with it anyway. *For roasting sweetcorn, see page 126.*

Autumn

Autumn is an indecisive beast. It can feel damp and spiderweb draped one day and as hot and dry as midsummer the next. At the beginning of the season, you think summer will never end, with sweetcorn, runner beans, tomatoes, courgettes (zucchinis), figs, raspberries, chard, aubergines (eggplants), blackberries, salad, chillis and sweet peppers reaching lush ripeness. But as the season cracks on, there's a chill in the evening air.

Even with crops in containers on a small balcony you'll begin to notice the change. While some, such as courgettes (zucchinis), runner beans and tomatoes, keep going for a month yet, others are starting to look a little tired, with leaves starting to yellow. But don't put away your garden trowel just yet. If you want fresh salads over winter and succulent broad (fava) beans next spring, this is the time to sow them while there's still warmth in the soil.

If you do only three things this season...

Sow broad (fava) beans, plant garlic, sow winter salad leaves

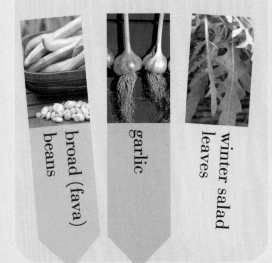

broad (fava) beans

garlic

winter salad leaves

Sow much to do...

It's also time to plant blackberries and raspberries for lush crops next year. And why not pop in some garlic and buy in some small plants of chard, either from garden centres or over the internet (*see Cheat's tip: a 'net result, below*)? With their vivid red, pink and orange stems, as lurid as highlighter pens, 'Bright Lights' chard shines as bright as a beacon in pots or borders as autumn moves on into winter.

All manner of wonderful salad crops can be sown or planted now – from winter lettuces to the watercress-like land cress, succulent winter purslane, lamb's lettuce and exotic-sounding oriental greens such as mizuna, mibuna and komatsuna, so good eaten raw, lightly steamed or added to stir-fries. Sown now or bought as ready-grown plants, you can be looking forward to virus-busting salads over the winter months (*see Weekend Project: A Spicy, Crunchy Salad Box for Winter, page 102*).

And don't forget the flowers. Spring wouldn't be the same without tulips and even a couple of pots on a balcony look glorious. Why not plant pure white or crimson red tulip bulbs in the same pots as salad – they look great standing sentry above a sea of frilly leaves. Alliums are another showstopper, especially the enormous Christophii, a ball of purple stars on a tall stem. Plant now in pots or garden beds for fireworks next summer. (*see Spring, Flowers to Include Just Because, page 61*).

Cheat's tip: a 'net result

Why be tied down to watering vulnerable seedlings you've sown yourself when you could let someone else do all the hard work for you? Most plant companies these days send out plants by post (*see Little Green Book, page 140*). Shopping this way is surprisingly addictive. I've spent many happy half-hours online browsing through photos of perfect chard and frilly lettuces when I should be working. Why not order some winter salad plants and chard now? Most even have 'winter collections' so you don't even need to choose specific plants. Once you've ordered, they'll email you to tell you when they've been despatched so you can arrange to be in. It's always worth asking the company to leave the package with a neighbour if you're out to save having to wait in post office queues. Hopefully your neighbour can read the instruction 'Live Plants' written on the side of the box and won't leave it under the stairs for two weeks before telling you. And to those sowing snobs who say, 'But aren't they expensive?' I'd say, 'What's better? Sowing loads of seedlings, spending lots of time watering them and then watching lots of them die because you went away for the weekend, or getting a handful of impeccably healthy plants through the door and planting them all in five minutes?'

Winter salad leaves

DIFFICULTY RATING

Growing winter salad leaves is great because you can indulge wildly in cakes, mince pies, chocolate and cheese over the Christmas period in the knowledge that tomorrow, when you feel utterly sick of stodge, you can pick a crisp, home-grown side salad and feel virtuous about yourself again. A salad dressed with a sweet honey and balsamic dressing to counteract the piquancy of some of these winter leaves is a wonderfully refreshing thing, and is particularly lovely when topped with some shavings of Parmesan or crumbles of creamy blue cheese *(see A Rather Decadent Winter Salad, page 117)*.

There are all sorts of delicious salad leaves you can sow in early autumn that will be ready to crop all through the winter and into next spring. It does have to be early autumn, mind you, when there's still warmth in the sun and soil and time for the plants to get to a decent size before winter stops them in their tracks.

These plants are all hardy – that is, they will survive frosts – though it's best to sow them in the warmest, most sheltered spots of your garden or to cover them with horticultural fleece *(see page 118)* to get the best out of them. If you're growing them in a container, place it in a sheltered spot. A window box of feathery green leaves is rather perky to look out on.

Unless stated otherwise below, thinly sow seeds direct into garden soil or a container filled with compost and barely cover with compost or soil. To harvest, either snip off individual leaves and add to salads – in which case the plant will resprout once or twice – or pull up whole plants.

For a really easy life, buy ready-grown plants, *see Cheat's tip: a 'net result, page 100.*

Winter purslane

A plant of many names – Claytonia perfoliata and miner's lettuce among them – this is a very pretty salad crop, with scallop-shaped, succulent leaves and stems with a refreshing, citrusy crunch. The leaves also have white flowers in the centre, like tiny jewels. The seeds are tiny, so don't do what I did first time and pour them all out on one spot by mistake. Mixing the seeds with a little sand helps to sow them further apart.

Mizuna

Feathery leaves rather like spikier, more robust rocket (arugula) works well as an edging for borders. Its flavour is also similar to rocket (arugula), though less spicy.

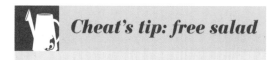

Cheat's tip: free salad

Winter purslane has a handy habit of seeding itself. Once sown and left to flower, it will pop up all over the place come spring next year. Don't weed these seedlings, leave them, and you'll have another crop of winter purslane to enjoy next autumn and winter.

Mibuna

Strap-like, narrow leaves and a similar taste to mizuna. Works well as a border.

Corn salad

Otherwise known as lamb's lettuce, this is an exceptionally hardy, low-growing, rosette-forming plant with a lovely mild flavour that counterbalances the pepperiness of many other salad leaves available at this time of year. No wonder it's a staple of shop-bought salad bags. It is, however, slow-growing, so don't expect to be eating it until spring.

Rocket (Arugula)

Not quite as hardy as the oriental leaves mizuna and mibuna, but worth trying an early autumn sowing.

Land cress

Exceptionally hardy salad plant with a taste almost identical to watercress. Serrated, low-growing leaves. Peppery, so use sparingly in salads.

Komatsuna

Tasting like a mix between cabbage and mustard, with a hint of spinach, this is a super-hardy, very useful salad leaf, which is also good in stir-fries.

Buckler-leaf sorrel

Delicious, tangy lemon taste and small, tender leaves. Ideal for adding to salads or, if left to mature, it makes a delicious soup.

Chervil

Herb with a delicate aniseedy taste and feathery leaves, delicious chopped and added to steamed carrots or broad (fava) beans. Sow in early autumn and you'll have these hardy leaves all winter. *See also page 32.*

Weekend Project: A Spicy Salad Box for Winter

This box of bountiful leafiness will keep you in refreshing, vitamin-packed salads and stir-fries however dark and short the winter days. Sown in early autumn, it will keep growing throughout the winter months and into the spring. Keep snipping off the leaves a couple of centimetres from soil level and each plant should recrop two or three times.

You will need
1 large window box with drainage holes
multipurpose compost
1 packet of oriental salad mix or oriental saladini
1 packet of winter purslane (Claytonia perfoliata) seeds
30 minutes

Add a layer of crocks to the bottom of the box and then fill it almost to the top with compost. Sprinkle your oriental salad mix thinly over the surface, leaving some space at each end. In this space, sprinkle the winter purslane seeds (beware, these are really tiny so this is best done a pinch at a time) as thinly as you can and then barely cover all with more compost and water.

Within ten days or so small shoots will begin to emerge. Oriental salad mixes usually contain a combination of mizuna, the feathery green salad leaf a little like rocket (arugula) though less spicy, mibuna (a non-feathery version), pak choi, red mustard, komatsuna and Chinese cabbage. Either snip the leaves off young, leaving a few centimetres above soil level so the plant can regrow, or wait until the leaves are a bit bigger and use them in a stir-fry.

A salad of these leaves with lardons of bacon and a creamy salad dressing to offset the pepperiness of some of the leaves is truly heavenly. The addition of the succulent, slightly lemony winter purslane gives the whole mix a welcome crunch.

Winter lettuce

It's lovely having a nice selection of well-flavoured, variously textured salad leaves, but they can seem a little insubstantial on their own. To make a really good winter salad you need some crunch and substance, too, and this is where winter lettuces come in.

I always sow a few in early autumn in plug trays to transplant when they are big enough. One of my favourites is 'Winter Density', a cos type with sweet, crunchy stems. Other good winter varieties include 'Black Seeded Simpson', which has pretty wrinkled leaves, 'Reine de Glace', with its robust yet mild-flavoured leaves, the sword-shaped 'Cocarde', the traditional soft round 'Valdor' and the beautifully coloured and very hardy 'Red Sails'.

All these lettuces are hardy and should survive outdoors all winter, but it has to be said that you'll get more tender leaves and faster growth if you put some fleece over them. I find the fleece tunnels brilliant – ready-made hoops with fleece attached that you can just concertina out into a tunnel and pop over a couple of decent rows. For plants in pots, you could wrap them in a fleece jacket (*see page 118*) instead. See Little Green Book, page 140 for garden equipment suppliers.

Sowing winter lettuces

When? Early autumn

Where? In module trays inside on a windowsill or outside in a sheltered spot.

YOU WILL NEED

A module tray, multipurpose compost, lettuce seeds, 20 minutes

How? Fill the module tray cells with compost and then tap the tray down gently to settle the compost and water so the surface of the compost is damp. Leave to drain for a couple of minutes, then place

Cheat's tip: a mixed blessing

You don't have to buy all these plants separately. You can buy collections of winter lettuce seedlings that you just unpack and pop into the soil. And packets of varied winter salad leaves, containing rocket, mizuna, mibuna, red mustards and pak choi are widely available. They're known as oriental salad mix or oriental saladini. Sow them direct into the soil or large containers in early autumn and crop until spring. *See Weekend Project: A Spicy, Crunchy Salad Box for Winter, page 102.*

two seeds on the surface of the compost in each cell and barely cover with compost.

What next? When the seedlings have germinated and are about 1 cm (½ in) high (a couple of weeks), pinch off the weaker seedling at soil level. Keep the compost moist and when the seedlings have six true leaves, plant out into your garden soil about 20 cm (8 in) apart. If growing in a pot, you can fit about five in a 30 cm (12 in) diameter pot. To harvest, either snip off individual leaves from the outside or leave the lettuces to heart up and cut the whole plant off at the base when mature.

Harvesting squashes and pumpkins

Your squashes and pumpkin vines should be trailing all over the place by autumn and have produced several decent-sized fruits. Leave them on the vines until mid-autumn but before the first frosts. Then cut them off. You could either then eat them straight away or, if you want to store them, leave them out in the sun for a few days to 'cure' (bring them inside at night if it's cold). This makes the skin nice and hard so preserves them for longer. You can then keep them over winter or cut little eyes and a mouth out of them for Halloween.

Speedy squash

For a gorgeous, super-fast lunch, take a squash (such as a butternut, 'Uchiki Kuri' or 'Blue Hubbard'), cut it in half and scoop out the seeds. Then put a wedge of butter in the middle, put the halves back together and pop in the microwave on high for about six minutes (checking it now and then to make sure it doesn't overcook). Season with salt and pepper and scoop straight out of the skin with a spoon.

Raspberries

DIFFICULTY RATING

If raspberry bushes were people, they'd be dependable sorts who would always turn up on time and never forget your birthday. They just get on with it, needing very little attention, but churning out their velvety berries for months, filling bowl after bowl. I planted three bushes (known as canes) in my garden two years ago and this year must have had enough raspberries to open a small farm shop.

For this reason alone – and, of course, the lush, juicy taste, but that goes without saying – raspberries are a good bet for a small edible garden owned by a busy person. They do need to be planted in garden soil, though, since their naturally spreading habit makes them unhappy in containers.

Unfortunately, the traditional way of growing raspberries seems to require an engineering degree and a very large tool kit. I'm talking of the dizzyingly sturdy post and wire support system that the books bang on about. I've tried this and the result was a bleak winter's evening with a power drill and a large stake, diminishing light and, eventually, tears. I'm not saying you're as rubbish as I am at DIY, but please. All you want to do is grow some berries, not construct an aerial assault course for paratroopers.

This is why I only grow 'Autumn Bliss' since, like all autumn-fruiting varieties, it needs no support and takes up less room. It's also dripping with berries in autumn when so much in the garden is beginning to wind up for the year. Other good autumn-fruiting varieties are 'Joan J' and the golden 'Fallgold'. You can buy 'Autumn Bliss' canes in pots in spring, but the usual time to plant them is as 'bare-rooted canes' in late autumn or winter. When these arrive, don't panic. They will look like something you'd throw for your dog in the park, but are actually alive.

And if you're worried that, by planting only an autumn-fruiting variety you're missing out on summer berries, think again … with a simple, nifty pruning tip, you can have raspberries from June to October *(see Cheat's tip: two crops from autumn-fruiting raspberries, page 116).*

Planting raspberries

When? Late autumn/winter

Where? Choose a sunny or partially shaded spot with well-cultivated soil that has preferably had lots of garden compost or well-rotted manure added to it.

YOU WILL NEED

Autumn-fruiting raspberry canes (three is enough for a small garden), 1 hour

How? Dig a hole big enough for the roots of the cane to spread out without cramping. Cover with soil, making sure that the soil level is the same as it was at the nursery (you should see a line on the cane where the soil came to). Repeat, spacing your canes about 50 cm (20 in) apart. With secateurs, now cut each cane back to about 20 cm (8 in) of the ground.

What next? Nothing until harvest time next year. For pruning of established bushes, *see Cheat's tip: two crops from autumn-fruiting raspberries, page 116.*

Where have I gone wrong? Raspberries don't get bothered by pests and diseases much, but might be attacked by aphids or raspberry beetle. *See Edible Garden Enemies, page 134.*

Bunging raspberries straight into my mouth in the garden is usually as far as I get when it comes to making fancy fruit puddings. But this lovely one occasionally tempts me into the kitchen. It looks far more la-di-dah than it actually is so could make someone special think you're marvellous. It can also be made with strawberries.

Serves 2
ready-made filo pastry, enough for 8 rectangles about 10 cm (4 in) by 5 cm (2 in)
200 ml (7 fl oz) double cream
250 g (8 oz) raspberries
icing sugar, for sprinkling
2 mint sprigs

Cut the pastry into rectangles using a sharp knife. Don't worry if they're not exactly the same size, we're not aiming for perfection. Lay them on greaseproof paper on a baking sheet and bake in a hot oven for 3–4 minutes or until they are crisp. Meanwhile, whip the cream.

When the pastry is cool, brush off any excess flour and layer them with the cream and raspberries between them, adding a generous sprinkle of icing sugar to each layer, making two stacks. Sprinkle more icing sugar on the top and pop a mint sprig on each if you're feeling particularly hostess-like. Serve immediately while the pastry is at its crispiest.

Blackberries

Why would you bother growing something that can rip your hands to pieces and that you can get for free from the grassy verges of most country lanes? It's a sensible question. So resistant have I always been to the thought of growing a cultivated strain of blackberry that it was only last year that one finally crept into my garden. But I'm now a total convert. First, they're one of the few edible crops that are happy growing up a shady wall – and how many urban gardeners among us have one of those? Second, you can buy thornless kinds that won't lacerate your fingers. Third, they can be trained in loop-the-loop shapes down the wall or fence, which looks rather pretty, even in winter. And fourth, the taste and size of some of these cultivated varieties puts their wild cousins to shame.

For ease of picking, choose a thornless variety such as 'Waldo' or 'Oregon Thornless', which has the added bonus of a fairly compact habit and pretty, dark green, parsley-like leaves.

Planting blackberries

When? Any time, though autumn gives the plant's roots plenty of time to establish before the growing season starts in spring

Where? Choose a sunny or shady spot near a fence with well-cultivated soil that has preferably had garden compost or well-rotted manure added

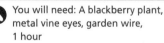

YOU WILL NEED

You will need: A blackberry plant, metal vine eyes, garden wire, 1 hour

How? Dig a hole big enough for the plant. Take it out of the pot and plant it in the hole. Fix your vine eyes to the wall or fence (if it's a fence you can simply screw them in by hand; if its a wall you may need to drill a hole and fit a Rawlplug into which to screw the vine eye). Then thread wire through them so that you end up with three parallel wires at roughly equal distance from each other up the fence.

What next? Keep the plant watered. Tie in new canes to the wires as they develop looping them up and down to keep them tidy. Blackberries grow in a fairly unusual way. In the first year, one or more long, loopy shoots will grow. Tie these in. In the second year, these shoots will bear fruit while the plant also puts out new shoots from the base that need tying in. To avoid getting all of these shoots into an unholy muddle, it's best to keep the old and new shoots separate, tying them in to different sides of the plant. The result is a really pretty and unusual-shaped plant. For pruning instructions, *see Pruning blackberries, page 114.*

Where have I gone wrong? Raspberry beetle is an occasional pest *(see Edible Garden Enemies, page 134).*

BRING IN THE HEAT LOVERS

As autumn gets into its stride, the days may still be warm and sunny, but the nights turn chilly. It's around this time that it's a good idea to bring the hot-blooded plants in pots in your garden inside to a sunny windowsill or room so that their fruits can ripen. Sweet peppers, chillis, aubergines (eggplants) and tomatoes will all benefit from this move to warmer climes.

It's also a good time to bring in your tender herbs to a sunny windowsill. Basil, mint, tarragon and chives can keep going right through winter if you do this. Bring in basil and tarragon plants in their pots. If your mint is planted in the soil, first cut back the dead, twiggy stems right down to ground level, then, using a hand trowel, dig up a patch of roots big enough for a medium-sized pot. Add compost to the bottom of the pot, then put the mint roots in and firm in, adding more compost if necessary. Water well. Within a week you'll see new green shoots coming up – perfect for making an impromptu mint sauce.

FIGS: YOU'VE GOT TO BE CRUEL TO BE KIND

Look, I know you won't want to hear this, but by mid-autumn, any figs that haven't already ripened won't.

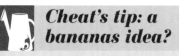

Cheat's tip: a bananas idea?

If your tomatoes are in pots that are too big to move and the fruits are still green by mid-autumn, they're unlikely to ripen this year. Cut the tomatoes off and place in a paper bag with a ripe banana. This gives off a plant-ripening hormone called ethylene, which helps ripen the tomatoes.

All they'll do is hang around, wasting the tree's energy, and then drop off. You've got to move on. Remove any figs that are cherry sized or bigger. Any that are smaller than this are the new figs that will develop next year so leave these. By late autumn/early winter, whenever the first frosts are drawing near, cover your tree with fleece to protect these embryo fruits from the cold. This gives them the very best chance of growing into lovely succulent fruits by next summer.

Broad (fava) beans

DIFFICULTY RATING

Hannibal Lecter has a lot to answer for. As if the 'fa-fa-fa-fava bean' didn't have enough of an image problem before he weighed in with his unusual cooking advice. The broad (fava) beans of my childhood were as appetizing as a plate of leathery, grey saddle-bags, but grow them yourself and a whole new world of broad (fava) bean opens up. Eat them small and sweet (*see A Salad to Put Spring in Your Step, page 52*) and they're absolutely delicious, full of the flavour of spring and with a gorgeous bright green vibrancy.

Hardy, hefty creatures, broad (fava) beans laugh in the face of frost and snow. Everything about them is reassuringly tough, from the enormous seeds that can be sown direct into garden soil to the pointy, grey-green leaves and clusters of pods that start to swell in mid-spring. They're a welcome splash of green over the winter months and plants produce their first delicious baby beans in late spring, when pickings from the garden are otherwise slim. I have been known to get so excited about this first new crop of the year that I pick them far too small and then lose them down the kitchen plug hole. Hopefully, you'll have more self-control.

The taller varieties have a tendency to flop about like the aftermath of a stag weekend, so tie them in to a wigwam or prop up with twiggy sticks. Alternatively, go for a dwarf variety such as 'The Sutton' that won't need any support – this is the one to choose for pots. If you want something different, the Crimson-flowered bean is rather beautiful, a heritage form with striking red flowers. Just make sure any seeds you sow at this point in the year are suitable for autumn sowing.

Sowing broad (fava) beans

When? Mid- to late autumn (you can also sow some varieties in spring, but I always think there's already enough to be getting on with at that time of year)

In pots

How? Add a layer of crocks to the bottom of the container and fill almost to the top with compost. Push in the seeds 5 cm (2 in) deep and about 10 cm (4 in) apart (or about five seeds to a 25 cm (10 in) pot). Water and place in a sunny, sheltered spot.

In garden soil

How? If using an obelisk, push it into the ground in a sunny, sheltered spot with well-cultivated soil. Sow about six seeds around the base of the obelisk 5 cm (2 in) deep. Water well. If using pea sticks as support, sow seeds 10 cm (4 in) apart, then push the sticks in among them.

What next? Green shoots should appear within 2–3 weeks, after which they'll need no real attention over the winter unless they're in pots, in which case you may need to water occasionally to stop them drying out. For more on broad (fava) beans, *see Cheat's tip: has beans, above right.*

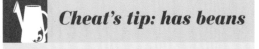

Cheat's tip: has beans

Broad (fava) beans that were sown in the autumn (*see page 106*) should be going great guns by mid-spring. Once the first pods have formed, pinch out the tips of the plants with your fingers. It stops the plants getting blackfly and the shoots are delicious steamed, tasting like a cross between beans and spinach.

What have I done wrong? Broad beans are tough brutes, but in the spring their tips do have a nasty habit of becoming infested with blackfly (*see Edible Garden Enemies, page 134*).

Garlic

When I was young I had a posh friend whose mother would waft around the garden in a floppy hat carrying a trug. I was deeply intimidated by her and her Brideshead vowels, but loved her kitchen, the ceiling of which was hung with dried herbs, onions and garlic, all gathered from her beautiful, walled kitchen garden. The whole room would be filled with the fragrance of drying rosemary and thyme, but it was the garlic, plaited and plump, that fascinated me most. It seemed so glamorous and foreign – the image of a more exotic climate.

I still think there's something wondrous about garlic, the way you pop one clove into the ground and it miraculously splits into a whole head of the stuff a few months later. But it couldn't be easier to grow, even in a northern European climate. Garlic must be a contender for the lowest-maintenance vegetable award. My own small urban garden keeps us self-sufficient in the stuff, and I still find something romantic about a bunch of my own dried garlic, dried earth still clinging to the roots, hanging from the cupboard door. Sometimes it even kids me into thinking I'm a good cook. There's a real pleasure in the ritual of prising out a clove, unwrapping the papery skin and chopping a bulb as the beginning to pretty much every dish – from pasta sauces to casseroles and soups.

Choose 'wet' or hardneck garlic such as 'Early Wight' or 'Purple Wight'. These don't keep for long but are ready by late spring and have a delicious mild, fresh flavour. Or go for the more common softneck kinds such as 'Solent Wight' that store for months, and the Elephant garlic (really a type of leek) with massive bulbs with a mild flavour. 'Albigensian Wight' from south-west France is a lovely, white-skinned bumpy one that keeps for ages.

Can't I just plant garlic from the supermarket?

Well, you could, but chances are it's been imported so won't be a variety that grows well in your climate. Better to buy from a garden centre or check out a specialist supplier – you'll also get a much wider choice of varieties that way *(see Little Green Book, page 140)*.

Planting garlic

When? Mid autumn to early winter

In pots

YOU WILL NEED

A container at least 45 cm (18 in) in diameter with drainage holes, multipurpose compost, garlic cloves, 20 minutes

How? Add a layer of crocks to the container and fill almost to the top with compost. Break the head of garlic up into cloves and push them into the compost flat end down so the pointy bit is just below the surface. Water and place in a sunny spot.

In garden soil

YOU WILL NEED

Garlic cloves, 15 minutes

How? Choose a sunny spot with well-cultivated soil. Garlic is happy in pretty much any soil, but does like good drainage so if you have a heavy clay, add a handful of horticultural sand or grit to the planting hole first. Plant as for pots, above.

What next? Over the next few weeks, you'll see the spiky green shoots come up – they'll provide welcome green over the winter and require nothing more from you until spring when they'll benefit from the odd watering. Dig up the garlic in the summer (or spring for very early varieties) after planting when the leaves start to yellow *(see Harvesting garlic, page 90)*.

Where have I gone wrong? Garlic is rarely troubled by pests and diseases though occasionally it suffers from white rot or rust. *See Edible Garden Enemies, page 134.*

Winter

It's the season of Christmas, radiators on full-blast, joining a gym and then going only once. It's a time to ignore the garden, isn't it? Well, you can if you want, but nature has a comforting way of never quite stopping the clock. It may not be the time for sowing anything much right now, but there are still things you could be picking – kale and chard for fire-side roast lunches, mizuna and mibuna for stir-fries, and chicory (endive), corn salad, winter purslane, rocket (arugula) and winter lettuce for salads so detoxifying and virtuous you can follow them with sticky toffee pudding and not hate yourself. And the benefit of growing it all outside your back door is, you only have to pop out into the cold for a moment to get it.

If you do only three things this season...

Plant a couple of fruit trees, buy seeds, order potatoes

fruit trees

buy seeds

order potatoes

Beat the cold, plant a tree

For the energetic, winter is the time to plant fruit trees. Even a tiny balcony has room for a couple of apples, a cherry or a plum. Or why not go a bit exotic with an apricot or peach? Fruit trees in pots are much easier to grow than you might think. As for me, as the winter weather bites, I'm usually to be found online, clicking through pictures of exotic chillis, weird-looking squashes and blue potatoes and dreaming about how amazing my garden is going to be next year. Again. Ordering seeds with your feet jammed into slippers shaped like rabbits might not be the height of glamour, but it beats moping on the sofa in front of the television.

Harvesting radicchio

Any radicchio you sowed back in the summer should be looking rather gorgeous by now, with deep burgundy, spiky leaves. I have a pot outside the back door and it really lifts the spirits on yet another glum mid-January day. You can either pick individual outer leaves to add to salads (be warned, they're quite bitter) or harvest the whole plant and grill it, which brings out the sweetness. Cut a whole radicchio head into quarters, brush with olive oil and grill it for a few minutes each side, then top with cheese and grill until the cheese bubbles.

Pruning blackberries

By winter, your blackberry bush will have finished fruiting. Using secateurs, cut down all the canes that had fruit on them this year. You will be left with a lop-sided bush, with all its canes trained over to one side. When the new canes start to develop in spring, simply tie them in to the other side to balance out the bush again. For planting blackberries, see page 106.

IT'S TIME TO PLANT FRUIT TREES

Don't think you need vast acres and a team of gardeners to produce delicious fruit from your garden. My little urban patch houses two pears, a plum, a fan-trained peach and apricot and two apple trees all in a space so small you could barely swing a chandelier. They're easier to grow than you might think.

The bare-root of the matter

Look, I know winter is probably the time you least feel like going outside and planting a fruit tree. It's cold, it's dirty and, anyway, the tree you ordered looks like a twig. But bear with me.

You can buy fruit trees all year round. A garden centre in midsummer will have pretty much any type of fruit tree for sale, all grown in pots. These are fine, but are sometimes dehydrated and pot-bound. You also won't get anywhere near the variety you would get from a specialist supplier. Order a bare-root tree online over the winter months *(see Little Green Book, page 140)* and you don't even have to cart anything into the back of the car. You'll get a far greater variety to choose from, they'll be much cheaper and probably healthier, too.

A bare-root tree is called that because it arrives looking like a tree that's been pulled out of the ground by a giant. Its roots dangle in midair and the branches look like something you'd put on the fire. But it's not dead, it's sleeping and, come spring, its leaves will unfurl. I did try telling that to a train-full of passengers when I took an apricot tree across London last winter, but they still looked at me like I'd escaped from a secure unit.

Growing fruit trees in pots

Minarette fruit trees are great for people with small gardens. They rather cleverly grow upright in a column shape with very short branches so you can plant them in pots and fit them into a small space like a terrace or balcony. You can get apples,

pears, cherries and plums grown this way. Why not get all four and have your own mini orchard?

Growing fruit trees against walls and fences

If you have a garden, why not try a beautiful ready-trained fruit tree? They come in some gorgeous shapes and look lovely even in winter. Cordons, shaped like acute accents, handsome multi-tiered espaliers, single-Us, fans … there are all sorts of fancy forms available that will love a warm wall or fence. They take years to get into these shapes and take some skill so buy them ready-trained unless you're a total masochist.

Apples and pears

DIFFICULTY RATING

They may not be exotic, but guess what, that means you're more likely to get a decent harvest. Good pear varieties include 'Concorde', 'Buerré Hardy' or 'Doyenné du Comice'. As for apples, there are so many varieties to choose from it's almost dizzying, but 'Discovery', 'Braeburn', 'Cox' and 'James Grieve' are all gorgeous. You might have to buy more than one tree for the best pollination – check with the suppliers.

Cheat's tip: two crops from autumn-fruiting raspberries

The usual way to prune autumn-fruiting raspberries is to cut all the canes down to the ground in late winter using secateurs. Since I'm a raspberry nut, however, I extend their fruiting season by pruning them slightly differently. In late winter, I cut only half the canes down to the ground. This way, I get raspberries in early summer as well as autumn.

A Rather Decadent Winter Salad

The slightly peppery winter salad leaves are a wonderful foil here for the lush creaminess of the blue cheese and sweetness of the dressing.

Serves 4 as a starter, 2 as a main
For the salad
3 good handfuls of winter salad leaves (lettuce, rocket (arugula), mizuna, chard … whatever you have growing out there), the larger leaves torn into pieces
1 head of forced Witloof chicory (endive), roughly sliced
100 g (3½ oz) Stilton cheese (or any creamy blue cheese)
1 and a half handfuls of pine kernels
For the dressing
1 tbsp cranberry sauce (from a jar)
½ tbsp red wine vinegar
½ tbsp balsamic vinegar
1 tbsp olive oil

Wash the salad leaves thoroughly and put in a large bowl. Add the chicory (endive) and then crumble the cheese on top. Put the pine nuts in a heavy-bottomed pan over a low heat for 3–4 minutes until they turn brown and are toasted, then sprinkle those on the top of the salad.

Put the cranberry sauce, vinegars and oil into a jam jar and give it all a good shake. Spoon it on top of the salad and toss well.

Plums and cherries

DIFFICULTY RATING

There's something so seductive about plums. They're no nonsense trees yet their fruits are full-fleshed sensuality itself. Eat them straight off the tree when they're still warm from the sun. Cherries are a great addition to a patio, too. 'Stella' and 'Sunburst' are good cherries, while, for plums, you really can't go wrong with the luscious 'Victoria'. You may have to chase the birds off, though – or protect with fleece when the fruits are at their ripest and most tempting. *See also A plum job, page 88.*

Jargon buster: horticultural fleece

Whenever a plant needs protecting against the cold – a lemon, peach or fig tree for example – you'll be advised to cover it with 'fleece'. The name conjures up images of sheep wool or the sort of thing you'd wear on ski lifts. And yet, horticultural fleece is a guazy, thin drape the consistency of a net curtain. How can this provide any protection against the biting cold of a winter's night? Well, it traps a thin layer of warmer air around the plant and this is, in most cases, enough to protect the vulnerable buds or shoots from damage. Or something along those lines …I just know it works. I wrap my fig and lemon tree in fleece jackets over winter. They have a drawstring and are really rather cute.

Peaches and apricots

Eating a sun-warmed, melting-fleshed, home-grown peach or apricot straight off the tree is perhaps the most fun you can have in the garden while sober. Bought peaches and apricots either seem to be as hard as billiard balls or with a texture and taste like cotton wool. But grow them yourself and they're in another league. I'm obsessed with my fan-trained 'Peregrine' peach and fuss around it like a window-dresser in a high-end department store. Buy a ready-trained fan and plant it in the soil or a pot against a sheltered, sunny fence or wall, training the branches into parallel wires. Alternatively, buy a dwarf tree and pop it in a pot in a sunny spot on your terrace.

There is, however, a big black mark against these luscious trees. From autumn to late winter you have to protect them with plastic to prevent peach leaf curl disease *(see Edible Garden Enemies, page 134)*, which can devastate crops. This can make your garden look like the store-room of a dry cleaner's. So delicious are the peaches, however, that I'm prepared to make this little sacrifice and, anyway, new resistant varieties are being bred all the time.

Go for white-fleshed 'Peregrine', the very reliable 'Rochester' and doughnut-shaped 'Saturn' with its honey-like taste. 'Bonanza' is particularly good in containers. As for apricots, you could do much worse than 'Moorpark', 'Aprigold' or 'Tomcot', which is particularly reliable in colder locations. *See also Cheat's tip: a tight fit for peaches, page 93.*

Entertaining

Call it inadequacy or rampant perfectionism, but cooking for more than two guests fills me with intense performance anxiety. Will the gravy taste of anything but stock powder? Will I unintentionally purée the broccoli again? Transfer the whole caboodle outside, however, and I magically transform into the hostess with the mostest, anticipating hordes of hungry guests with nothing but pleasure, like a cut-price Martha Stewart. What is it about eating outside that brings out the carefree in even the most hopeless of hosts? Usually a slave to a recipe, I only need a whiff of an al fresco grill and I'm throwing salads, marinades and impromptu puddings together with happy abandon. And if a couple of sausages fall through the barbecue grill and turn to charcoal, who cares?

If you do only three things ...

Throw home-grown sweetcorn on the barbie; make a herb marinade; rustle up a mean mojito

sweetcorn

herb marinate

mojito

Let's go outside...

It's like when you were at school and the teacher said, 'It's too hot, we're going to work outside today', which, as everyone knew, was a signal to gossip, draw on your hands in biro and daydream to the hazy backdrop of someone mowing grass. It's the same when eating outside. Normal rules don't apply. People get up halfway through their meal to poke the barbecue. Everyone's in and out of the kitchen carrying bowls. Someone's dropped the potato salad in the dahlias. No one is paying so much attention to the food because it shares double-billing with the sunshine and general charmingness (you hope) of your surroundings. But, if they were, it wouldn't matter, because, as everyone knows, food tastes better when you eat it outside. And when that food includes tomatoes, herbs, garlic, new potatoes, peppers, courgettes and strawberries that you've just picked feet away from the table, it tastes better than ever.

So how do you make your outside dining experience as glorious as possible? A little attention to outside lighting, seating and decoration can turn even the most humdrum of balconies or terraces into twinkling, magical wonderlands you won't want to leave until the wee small hours. Tear herbs and throw them straight into salads after a quick rinse under the garden tap. Eat strawberries straight from the plant after a quick dip in some whipped double cream. After all, where better to enjoy the fruits of your labours but in their natural setting?

THE BARBECUE

Don't believe what your dad/boyfriend/husband tells you. Barbecuing is not a science requiring a post-grad degree, starched chef's hat and gleaming set of different-sized tongs. It's a question of lighting the corner of a paper bag and walking away, then coming back about half an hour later with a herby lamb chop. Barbecues have moved on from the old days when men (for it was ever thus) fiddled around with charcoal that never seemed to light until all the guests were so drunk they had to go home.

For we now have 'instant lighting' charcoal that comes in its own handy paper bag. So wondrous is this product that you don't even have to touch the charcoal, just light the corner of the bag with a match and the whole thing slumps to perfect, cookable-on embers.

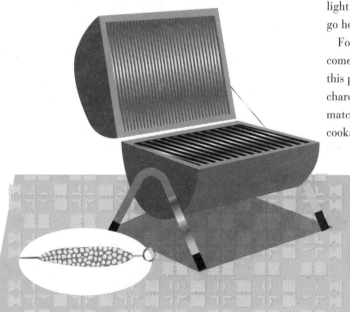

These days you can buy rather stylish barbecue sets too: little silver, blue or pink numbers so cute you want to pat them. Or gorgeous braziers (I'm currently in love with mine) that cook a steak beautifully, but that you can also burn logs in. Sit around it, toast marshmallows and warm your hands when the night turns chilly. And don't knock those disposable foil barbecue sets you can

Cheat's tip: herby embers

Throw twigs of fresh rosemary or thyme onto the barbecue embers and fill the air with a delectable herby scent. The oils will flavour the food too.

get in garages and supermarkets. Despite what barbecue snobs may say, they work just fine and you won't even have to clean the grill pan afterwards.

Marinades

Garden herbs are fantastic for making marinades for barbecue meats. They can transform a steak or lamb chop into something delectable in an hour. Woody, robust herbs such as thyme, oregano and rosemary when mixed with garlic, lemon juice and olive oil are always a winner. Rosemary goes particularly well with lamb, thyme with chicken, and oregano with grilled halloumi cheese for your veggie guests. All these herbs are easily grown in pots (*see Herbs, page 30*). Use a pestle and mortar to bash the woody herbs up a bit to release their oils. Lay your barbecue meat in the mixture in a bowl for at least an hour – overnight gives a real chance for the flavours to penetrate – and then put it on the grill.

Herbs for salads

Other, less woody herbs such as parsley, coriander, basil, mint, chervil and chives are worth their weight in gold, too. Tomato salad is an adaptable beast – when eaten with basil it tastes totally different to the way it does with coriander or parsley. Try mixing up red and orange cherry tomatoes, topped with buffalo mozzarella and torn basil. Mint leaves are delicious with fresh peas, baby broad beans or warm, freshly dug new potatoes, and a potato salad just isn't the same without a generous handful of chopped chives.

Quick, Easy and Delicious Bruschetta

A gorgeous way to show off the flavour of just-picked, home-grown tomatoes, and one of my favourite edible garden recipes. Its also makes the most of other crops you could be growing such as garlic and basil. Quickly thrown together and irresistibly moreish.

Serves 4 as a generous snack
4 ciabatta rolls
2 garlic cloves
extra virgin olive oil
4 or 5 handfuls of freshly picked tomatoes
1 handful of freshly picked basil leaves
sea salt and freshly ground black pepper

Slice the ciabattas in half and toast them lightly. Then rub one side of each with a garlic clove (using the bread almost like a grater). Drizzle over a little olive oil. Chop the tomatoes finely (no need to skin them) and heap them on top of the slices, then top with torn basil leaves. Drizzle with more olive oil and season with salt and pepper.

Serve outside with cold white wine on a hot day.

More home-grown al fresco gorgeousness

There are loads of ways a barbecue can make the most of your freshly picked fruit and vegetables. How about kebabs of courgette, sweet pepper, onion, aubergine and halloumi cheese? A warm salad of just-dug new potatoes and broad beans? Or baby beetroot roasted in foil served with a thick dip of crème fraîche and chives? For pudding, there might be raspberries, strawberries or blueberries. For the easiest dish, throw them onto shop-bought meringues with whipped double cream. Or, if you're feeling a bit more fancy, sandwich them between layers of crisp filo pastry and whipped cream *(see Crisp Raspberry and Cream Stacks, page 105)*.

Say it with flowers

You've gone to the trouble of making a salad. Why not throw a few vividly coloured, edible petals on top? They bring a subtle peppery flavour and look irresistible. You don't need many petals – four or five nasturtiums and a couple of heartsease violas or borage flowers, say, is enough. *See Edible flowers, page 60.*

Sweetcorn

Sweetcorn *(see page 50 and 92)* is not the easiest crop to grow in a northern European climate. But if you get it right, you're in for a proper treat on barbecue night. In fact, I'd go so far as to say it's worth scheduling a barbecue entirely around your sweetcorn harvest, so delicious is it when freshly roasted on the grill. Simply pull a cob off the plant, husks, silks and all and submerge in cold water for at least an hour. Shake to drain and then place on the grill for 20 minutes, turning occasionally. Remove the husk and silk before eating with plenty of butter, salt and freshly ground black pepper.

The Very Freshest Tzatziki

This is a great impromptu dip to bring out when you have a few friends over. It's also delicious with barbecued meat such as lamb chops. It only takes about 15 minutes to make.

Serves 4–6
3 home-grown cucumbers, picked small
(about 10 cm/4 in long)
250 ml (8 fl oz) Greek yogurt
1 generous handful of freshly picked mint,
stems removed and leaves
chopped
1 garlic clove, crushed
couple of squeezes of
lemon juice, optional

Peel the cucumbers and then half them lengthways. Remove the seeds and then grate or finely chop the flesh. Pour the yogurt into a bowl and mix in the other ingredients, including the cucumber. Serve with raw carrots, breadsticks, mini falafels or toasted wedges of pitta bread or with roast pork or lamb.

AL FRESCO DINING IN STYLE

Any outside space can be transformed into a den of dining loveliness. The only thing that really matters is that you feel comfortable. After all, you're not going to have a rip-roaring evening if your guests' buttocks have gone to sleep on a cast-iron filigree chair, however elegant it is. I've had perfect evenings lounging on cushions on a rug with garden flares pushed into pots nearby as light. So dégagé was the scene that a guitar may even have been produced at some point, about which probably the less said the better.

Furniture-wise, I always think the light is best so you're not restricted to one place. Bistro-style sets – round metal folding tables and wooden slatted chairs – are cheap, stylishly simple and can be left outside all winter. Ugly plastic tables can be covered with throws

Here's one I grew earlier

It's not that you're a show-off, of course, but really what is the point in growing a lemon or fig tree if your guests can't be suitably impressed by their fragrant exoticism and your obvious gardening know-how? So make sure they're near the table. The scent of citrus blossom is particularly lovely, especially if you haven't masked it with the whiff of burning lamb chops. And if you have actually managed to grow a lemon (*see Lemons, page 94*) this would be the time to pick it, slice it and add it to Gin and tonic. As for a fig tree, a handsome potted specimen next to the table instantly transports you to the Mediterranean, even if it is a typical British summer's day – grey and just about to drizzle.

or tablecloths and chairs with colourful cushions. Director's-style folding chairs are great – comfortable, cheap and easy to fold away at the end of the summer. Deckchairs never seem to date. Outdoor beanbags are fun and super comfortable, come in seductive colours, are water-resistant and the perfect place to digest the Sunday papers. It takes temptation indeed to coax me from my pink lounger-style beanbag from June to September. You can buy outdoor cushions with plasticated backs so they don't get damp – but indoor ones will do just as well, as long as you remember to bring them in before the dew and don't agonize too much if they get ketchup on them.

Tripping the light fantastic?

Who hasn't spent an evening holding their fork over a tea light in the hope of seeing whether any slugs have climbed on with the potato salad? Yes, garden lighting has to be strong enough to let you see what you're eating, but only just. You don't want to feel you're eating in a bus station. Candles, flares and fairy lights are your twinkly friends.

I'm a big believer in more is more in the candle

department, which is another way of saying, I'm a tea-light junkie. I buy big bags of them and dot them around the table and all over the garden in jam jars or little lanterns, hanging them from walls, trees and the pergola. Of course this means that I then spend much of the evening dashing round replacing the things when they burn out, but, I tell myself, it's a small price to pay for ambience. Garden flares are even easier because they burn happily for hours. Just don't stick them too near your plants or they'll go up in smoke – that lovely herby fragrance you think is the steak marinade might just be your prize bay tree. On the table, I go for a couple of massive white candles placed in hurricane glasses to stop them blowing out in the slightest breeze.

But the easiest way of all to transform a dingy terrace is good old fairy lights. Wrap them in the branches of trees, around balconies, hang them on an outside wall. You can't really go wrong with these, unless you leave the flex across a doorway and hospitalize your guests. Coloured ones have a certain Greek taverna appeal. Kitsch queens might like lights shaped like chillis or made up of fabric flowers. But for most of us, simple white lights are just perfect.

And for my next trick...

If you're drinking white wine, try popping a borage flower into each glass at the table at the last minute. The blue star-shaped flowers turn a beautiful pink when they come into contact with the acid in the wine.

A Mojito to banish a day at the office

A holiday in Cuba a few years ago left me so unimpressed with the island's cuisine that I left seven pounds lighter (that'll be dry chicken with boiled rice and half a tomato again, then). Still, all wasn't lost – I began a love affair with its famous cocktail. Grow mint yourself and you can always be an arm's length away from some Caribbean escapism. And you won't even have to eat the food.

Makes 1 glass
14 fresh mint leaves, plus a sprig to decorate –
garden mint
(Mentha spicata), otherwise known as
spearmint, is best, but any will do
1½ tsp white sugar (preferably caster)
juice of ½ a lime
4 large ice cubes
2 measures (50 ml/2 fl oz) light rum
2 splashes of angostura bitters (not essential,
but they do add a lovely flavour)
sparkling mineral water

Put the mint leaves, sugar and lime juice in a tumbler glass and bash it all together a bit with a fork or spoon to bring out the mint flavour. Fill the glass with crushed ice (either bash your ice cubes in a pestle and mortar or put them in a tea towel and crush with a rolling pin). Add the rum and angostura bitters, and top with sparkling water and a sprig of mint.

A Fruitful Pimm's

You don't need to be punting down a river to enjoy the definitive drink of summer. It's a great way to show off your gorgeous strawberries, cucumber, mint and borage flowers. Don't overdo the bits, though, you don't want to feel like you're drinking a meadow.

Serves 6
Pimm's No. 1 cup
1 large bottle of lemonade
1 small home-grown cucumber
(or one-third of a shop-bought one)
2 handfuls of freshly picked strawberries
freshly picked mint sprigs
about 10 borage flowers
(see Edible flowers, page 60)
plenty of ice cubes

Mix 1 part Pimm's to 4 parts lemonade in a large jug, leaving one-third of the space at the top to allow for the fruit. Slice the cucumber thinly lengthways (or across if a larger shop-bought one). Halve or quarter the strawberries, depending how big they are. Add the ice cubes, strawberries, cucumber and mint and give it all a quick stir. Finally, add the borage flowers on the top and serve.

AL FRESCO DRINKS FOR PARTY TIME

Very nice ice

If, after making your cocktails, your hostess-with-the-mostest zeal still isn't spent, why not really push the boat out? Freeze edible flowers (*see below*) in ice cubes and add them to cocktails, fruit juices or just plain water in a jug. Your friends will be floored with admiration as they see perfect orange nasturtiums and viola flowers, suspended in pure ice, floating in their glass. Either that or they'll think something has fallen in from the shrubbery.

The only slightly odd thing about making these rather exquisite ice cubes is that you have to use distilled water. Otherwise, the ice cube goes all cloudy, which ruins the effect. Buy distilled water from supermarkets or garages and then half fill an ice-cube tray with it and freeze. Pick a few nasturtiums, violas, borage flowers, raspberries, blueberries, sprigs of mint or anything else in the garden you think will look nice and lay them on the ice, then fill to the top with more distilled water and freeze. And there you go, beautiful ice cubes to make any drink a work of art. Bree Van de Kamp would be proud of you.

The morning after

Over-indulged the night before? Relocate your inner peace and clear your head with some herbal brews. Try putting five or six rosemary leaves in the bottom of a cup and pouring on boiling water. Leave for a few minutes and then drink. A lemon verbena tea will also banish the cobwebs. Pour boiling water over five or six leaves and leave for a few minutes before drinking – preferably in a dark room. If this still doesn't work, make yourself a bacon sandwich and take a Paracetamol.

Edible garden enemies

It's unfortunate, but you won't be the only one wanting to eat the fruit and vegetables you grow. There's a legion of pests out there – slugs and snails, mainly – who fancy their chances too, and a few diseases that could get in the way of you and edible perfection. We've all been tempted to reach for the slug pellets of doom and the sprays of certain insect annihalation on discovering a broad bean plant swarming with blackfly or a snail trail where treasured carrot seedlings were yesterday, but how do you cope with pests and diseases if you want to garden organically? Armed with vigilance, insecticidal soft soap and a good squishing finger, you should get the better of the beasts and other ills that can affect your precious specimens. All the disease and pest deterrents listed are organic.

If you do only three things ...

Buy insecticidal soft soap and a plastic spray bottle; lay twiggy sticks over soil to keep cats away; remember, slugs and snails are your enemies

insecticidal soft soap

keep cats away

stop slugs and snails

Aphids

See Greenfly and Blackfly, below.

Blackfly

A particular pest of beans – broad, runner and French – these tiny black flies swarm over the growing tips, sucking the sap. You'll often see ants 'farming' them by stroking them to release the sap, which they then eat. In broad beans, the way to avoid blackfly is to pinch out the growing tips of the plants once four trusses of pods have formed. You can eat the tips steamed – they taste rather good, like spinach. Otherwise, either blast off the flies with a jet of water or spray with insecticidal soft soap solution, an organic aphid deterrent available from all garden centres. Buy a cheap, plastic spray bottle to apply it with.

You could also try diluting a couple of drops of washing-up liquid in a spray bottle and spraying that on for similar results.

Blight

This is a serious fungal disease that affects potatoes and tomatoes. The first signs in potatoes are brown patches on the leaves with white rings around them on the undersides. In tomatoes, similar brown patches appear on the leaves, with blackened patches on the stems. Unfortunately, once the disease has taken hold, there's very little you can do so it's best to plant blight-resistant varieties. Cut affected potato leaves down to the ground and burn them immediately in the hope that the spores have not yet infected the potato tubers in the ground. With tomatoes, whole crops of fruit can turn black and rotten almost overnight. The disease is worse in damp, cool summers. The good news is that if you only grow first or second early potatoes you are unlikely to be troubled by it.

Blossom end rot

A disease in tomatoes in which a leathery, dark patch appears at the bottom of the fruit. It's caused by irregular watering. Remove any affected fruits and take care to water little and often rather than via an occasional deluge.

Botrytis

Fruits or leaves develop a grey, furry mould that spreads until the whole fruit rots. It's worse during a wet summer. Remove any infected fruit and leaves. When planting lettuces don't bury the leaf bases under the soil.

Carrot fly

A serious pest of carrots, these flies lay eggs that hatch into maggots and tunnel into the centre of your carrots causing them to rot. Telltale signs are reddish leaves that wilt in sunny weather. Your only solution to this problem is prevention: the best way is to grow varieties with built-in carrot fly resistance *(see page 41)*; you can also grow carrots in

containers more than 60 cm (2 ft) above ground
level (the flies are lazy fliers); finally, make sure you
sow thinly so that you don't have to thin the carrots
later, the smell of which can attract the flies.

Caterpillars

Large holes in your kale or nasturtium leaves? No
slug or snail trails? Look for caterpillars, the most
likely culprit. Remove any you see and squash them,
and look out for egg clusters on the underside of the
leaves and squash these too.

Cats

See Edible garden public enemy no. 2, page 51.

Common scab

A disease often seen on potatoes in which scabby,
scurfy patches appear on the surface of the tubers.
It's only skin deep and doesn't affect the taste so
simply scrub off the patches and eat as normal.

Flea beetle

Rocket leaves peppered with tiny holes? A cloud of tiny black beetles that fly up when you disturb the leaves? You have flea beetles. A mild infestation doesn't really do your crop any harm, and you won't even notice the little holes in your salad, but if you're worried, avoid growing rocket between late May and midsummer since this is the period when thee little charmers are most around.

Greenfly

Like blackfly, these congregate on the soft growing tips of young plants, sucking the sap and weakening the plants. The sap they excrete also coats the surface of the plant with a horrible stickiness that encourages fungal diseases. It is best to get rid of them when you see them. Spray with insecticidal soft soap solution or a few drops of washing-up liquid diluted in a spray bottle.

Peach leaf curl

This is the curse of peaches, apricots and nectarines, a fungal disease that is spread by rain splash. For this reason, the recommended prevention is to cover your tree with plastic from autumn to late winter. Admittedly, it's not pretty, but as someone who has lost an entire peach crop to the dreaded lurgy, I'm happy to drape away. Signs of the disease are red, puckered leaves in spring, which later fall off.

Powdery mildew

Does it look as though someone has dipped your plant's leaves in talcum powder? Sounds like powdery mildew, a fungal disease caused by bad ventilation, not enough moisture in the soil and damp air. It's particularly common in peas, courgettes, squashes and sweet peas and, although unlikely to kill a plant, does weaken it, reduce cropping and make it look rather grim. Prevent in the first place by not overcrowding your plants. If you have it, try diluting one part milk to nine parts water and spraying the liquid onto the leaves. Also keep plants well watered and fed and try to increase ventilation around the plant as much as you can.

Raspberry beetle

A pest of raspberries and blackberries that lays its eggs inside the fruit, making them brown, hard and inedible. You might find little white grubs in the berries. If you think you've got this pest, immerse the berries in salty water to bring out any unwelcome guests and then rinse them under cold water before eating.

Red spider mite

Usually only seen in indoor plants or outside in particularly hot summers where the dry air encourages these microscopic insects to colonize the leaves and suck the sap. It can be a problem for peppers, cucumbers and lemon trees. Telltale signs are white web fibres and pale yellow dots on the underside of the leaves. Mist the leaves regularly to keep up humidity. Indoors, a biological control called Phytoseiulus persimilis can be effective.

Rust

Orange spots on the leaves of garlic. If you see it, harvest your garlic as usual but don't plant it in the same spot for three years.

Scale insect

This is a problem for citrus trees. Little shield-like bugs cluster on the undersides of the leaves and in the joints where the leaves meet the stems and suck the sap, weakening the tree. Remove them by hand or with an old toothbrush and soapy water.

Slugs and snails

See Edible Garden public enemy no. 1, page 36.

Split tomatoes

This is also caused by irregular watering. Take care to water little and often rather than via an occasional deluge.

Whitefly

If you see clouds of tiny white moths that fly up from plants when disturbed, chances are you have whitefly. They weaken the plants, and can be a particular problem with young tomato seedlings. Spray with insecticidal soft soap solution or a few drops of washing up liquid diluted in a spray bottle.

White rot

A disease affecting the roots of the allium family – leeks, onions and garlic – that eventually rots the crop. Telltale signs are fluffy white mould in the soil around the roots and a sickly, yellowing and wilted plant. Dig up and burn affected plants and don't plant alliums in the same place for at least three years until the disease has left the soil.

The Little Green Book

Plants, trees and seeds

Crocus

www.crocus.co.uk

The first major online plant and gardening equipment supplier and still hard to beat for reliability and range. Their instant herb garden, salad garden and vegetable garden collections are the ultimate in lazy kitchen gardening and they do a nice line in stylish pots, obelisks and garden furniture, too.

Delfland Nurseries

www.organicplants.co.uk

Very handy company that sends small vegetable and salad plants through the post. Simply open the parcel and plant.

D.T. Brown

www.dtbrownseeds.co.uk

Good online fruit and vegetable seed and plant supplier.

The Garlic Farm

www.thegarlicfarm.co.uk

Garlic grower and supplier of a wide variety of garlic bulbs based on the Isle of Wight.

Jekka's Herb Farm

www.jekkasherbfarm.com

The online nursery of the woman Jamie Oliver has

called 'the Queen of herbs' is the definitive port of call if you want to know your Morrocan mint from your Pineapple or source some delectable Thai basil.

Keepers Nursery

www.keepers-nursery.co.uk

They call themselves the leading specialist fruit tree nursery in the UK and who am I to argue? These people are fruit gurus. Their website is fantastic for any fruit tree or bush. They take orders throughout the year, but only deliver in the dormant season between November and March.

Ken Muir

www.kenmuir.co.uk

Leading online supplier of fruit plants, bushes and trees. The place to go to buy strawberry plants, raspberry canes and fruit trees, and a mine of information for choosing trees, pruning and other advice.

The Organic Gardening Catalogue

www.organiccatalog.com

Wide range of organic and heritage vegetable seeds as well as gardening equipment.

The Real Seed Collection

www.realseeds.co.uk

A lovely online seed company run by a couple in Wales who try out all the varieties of seed they sell at home. The website has a similarly refreshing, home-made feel. They specialize in rare, heritage varieties and all are non-hybrid.

Sarah Raven's Kitchen & Garden

www.sarahraven.com

Online nursery of the British gardening personality who specializes in attractive and heritage flower, vegetable and salad seeds and has some ingenious time-saving collections such as 'Foodies tomato seedlings'. The place to go for edible flower seeds.

Seeds of Italy

www.seedsofitaly.com

Looking at the online catalogue of this Italian seed company is almost as good as getting on a plane to Tuscany...gorgeous squashes, tomatoes, peppers and salad seeds to bring some sun-baked flavour to your garden.

Thompson & Morgan

www.thompson-morgan.com

Online seed and plant company, with a particular speciality in potatoes.

Tuckers Seeds

www.tuckers-seeds.co.uk

Great selection of good-value vegetable seeds. Their packets of seeds are often bigger than those of other suppliers. The best choice for value, though a small garden may not need quite so many seeds.

Garden accessories, equipment and furniture

Crocus

See p.140.

Garden Boutique

www.gardenboutique.co.uk

Stylish gloves, hats, aprons and wellies. The place to go for a set of nifty little tools so cute you won't want to hide it under the stairs.

Harrod Horticultural

www.harrodhorticultural.com

Great for any gardening equipment from automatic watering systems to tools, greenhouses and cloches.

Hen & Hammock

www.henandhammock.co.uk

Online den of horticultural loveliness specializing in gardening things made from recycled materials – from stylish tyre trugs to glass bell cloches.

Plantstuff

www.plantstuff.co.uk

Chic online garden furniture and accessories company. Slate seed labels, bird tables, cloches, olde worlde wooden seed trays, antique galvanized pots, leather kneelers … all the stuff you may not strictly need for your garden, but that you really want all the same.

The Urban Garden

www.theurbangarden.co.uk

Garden equipment, furniture and lighting for city livers with sophisticated tastes. Particularly good for window boxes and ingenious planters, such as their handsome recycled tyre pots and pretty willow surround planters – perfect for brightening up a windowsill.

Wiggly Wigglers

www.wigglywigglers.co.uk

Colourful and cheerful online business specializing in groovy beehive compost bins – pink or baby blue anyone? – bokashi and wormery systems and charming bird boxes and feeders. They also sell seeds and tools.

Index

Acknowledgements

To D, of course.

Thanks also to my mum, my in-laws, my neighbour Ellie and anyone else who helped give me five minutes to write this among a cacophony of small children and builders. Thanks to Heather Holden-Brown and Elly James for their calm advice. Also thanks to David Hews for shooting the cover and The Creaky Shed and The Deptford Project for their assistance. Thanks, finally, to Emma and Amy at New Holland for making it all into a proper book.